130-
24F

The Economics and Mathematics of Aggregation: Formal Models of Efficient Group Behavior

The Economics and Mathematics of Aggregation: Formal Models of Efficient Group Behavior

P. A. Chiappori

Columbia University
USA
pc2167@columbia.edu

Ivar Ekeland

University of British Columbia
Canada
ekeland@math.ubc.ca

the essence of knowledge

Boston – Delft

Foundations and Trends® in Microeconomics

Published, sold and distributed by:
now Publishers Inc.
PO Box 1024
Hanover, MA 02339
USA
Tel. +1-781-985-4510
www.nowpublishers.com
sales@nowpublishers.com

Outside North America:
now Publishers Inc.
PO Box 179
2600 AD Delft
The Netherlands
Tel. +31-6-51115274

The preferred citation for this publication is P. A. Chiappori and I. Ekeland, The Economics and Mathematics of Aggregation: Formal Models of Efficient Group Behavior, Foundations and Trends® in Microeconomics, vol 5, nos 1–2, pp 1–151, 2009

ISBN: 978-1-60198-288-9

Editorial Scope

Foundations and Trends® in Microeconomics will publish survey and tutorial articles in the following topics:

- Environmental Economics
- Contingent Valuation
- Environmental Health Risks
- Climate Change
- Endangered Species
- Market-based Policy Instruments
- Health Economics
- Moral Hazard
- Medical Care Markets
- Medical Malpractice
- Insurance economics
- Industrial Organization
- Theory of the Firm
- Regulatory Economics
- Market Structure
- Auctions
- Monopolies and Antitrust
- Transaction Cost Economics
- Labor Economics
- Labor Supply
- Labor Demand
- Labor Market Institutions
- Search Theory
- Wage Structure
- Income Distribution
- Race and Gender
- Law and Economics
- Models of Litigation
- Crime
- Torts, Contracts and Property
- Constitutional Law
- Public Economics
- Public Goods
- Environmental Taxation
- Social Insurance
- Public Finance
- International Taxation

Information for Librarians

Foundations and Trends® in Microeconomics, 2009, Volume 5, 8 issues. ISSN paper version 1547-9846. ISSN online version 1547-9854. Also available as a combined paper and online subscription.

Foundations and Trends® in
Microeconomics
Vol. 5, Nos. 1–2 (2009) 1–151

DOI: 10.1561/0700000028

now
the essence of knowledge

The Economics and Mathematics of Aggregation: Formal Models of Efficient Group Behavior

P. A. Chiappori[1] and Ivar Ekeland[2]

[1] *Columbia University, USA, pc2167@columbia.edu*
[2] *University of British Columbia, Canada, ekeland@math.ubc.ca*

Abstract

The goal of this article is to provide a general characterization of group behavior in a market environment. A crucial feature of our approach is that we do not restrict the form of individual preferences or the nature of individual consumptions; we allow for public as well as private consumption, for intragroup production, and for any type of consumption externalities across group members. Our only assumption is that the group always reaches Pareto efficient decisions.

We analyze two main issues. One is testability: what restrictions (if any) on the aggregate demand function characterize the efficient behavior of the group? The second question relates to identifiability; we investigate the conditions under which it is possible to recover the underlying structure — namely, individual preferences, the decision process and the resulting intragroup transfers — from the group's aggregate behavior.

Our approach applies to large (markets) or small (households) groups, with both private and public consumptions, with and without restrictions on trade, with monetary or real endowments. In particular, our approach generalizes the classical analysis of the aggregate demand of a market economy, as pioneered by Gerard Debreu, Ralph Manted and Hugo Sonnenchein; we devote a section of our work to this specific but important case.

We show that in all these contexts, aggregation of individual behaviors involves a common mathematical structure, whereby the aggregate demand of the group, considered as a vector field, can be decomposed into a sum of gradients. The proper way to understand this structure, and ultimately to find necessary and sufficient condition for such a decomposition to be possible, is to use tools which were developed about 100 years ago, mainly by the French mathematician Elie Cartan, and which are known now-a-days as exterior differential calculus (EDC). The last section of this article is devoted to an exposition of EDC and contains the proofs of the results in the preceding ones.

Contents

1

Introduction

The study and characterization of economic behavior in a market context is one of the goals of microeconomic theory. Most existing results concentrate on two extreme cases. One is individual behavior. It has been known for at least one century that individual demand, as derived from the maximization of a single utility function under budget constraint, satisfies specific and stringent properties (homogeneity, adding up, Slutsky symmetry and negativeness). The alternative case concerns the aggregate behavior of a large number of agents. The main conclusion of the so-called Debreu–Mantel–Sonnenschein (henceforth DMS) literature[1] is that, if the number of agents exceeds the number of commodities, aggregate (excess) demand does not exhibit specific properties, except for the obvious ones (continuity, homogeneity, Walras Law). In other words, the standard assumptions of microeconomic theory generate considerable structure at the individual level, but this structure is essentially lost by (large) aggregation.

However, many interesting economic situations lie somewhere in-between these two polar situations. These are cases where the group

[1] See Shafer and Sonnenschein (1982) for a general survey.

under consideration includes more than one individual, but is not large enough for the aggregation results of DMS type to apply. For instance, standard demand theory uses data on households or families, most of which gather several individuals. The behavior of even large firms is routinely analyzed as stemming from the interaction of a small number of agents (management and unions, manager and shareholders, top manager and division heads, etc.), who bargain under some global financial constraint. The same remark obviously applies to committees, clubs, villages and other local organizations, who have also attracted much interest. In short, many economic decisions are made by small, multi-person groups.

The goal of this book is to provide a general characterization of group behavior in a market environment. The general problem we consider can be stated as follows. Consider a group consisting of S members. The group has limited resources; specifically, its global consumption vector ξ must satisfy a standard market budget constraint of the form $p^{\mathrm{T}}\xi = y$ (where p is a vector of prices and y is total group income). Any demand vector belonging to the global budget set thus defined can be consumed by the members. Some of the goods can be privately consumed, while others may be publicly used. Empirically, the intragroup allocation of resources or consumptions is not observable; the group is perceived as a 'black box', and only its *aggregate* behavior, summarized by the demand function $\xi(p,y)$, is recorded. A crucial feature of our approach is that we do *not* restrict the form of individual preferences (except for the standard convexity assumptions) or the nature of individual consumptions. That is, we allow for public as well as private consumption, for intragroup production, and for any type of consumption externalities across group members. What restrictions (if any) on the aggregate demand function characterize the efficient behavior of the group? And when is it possible to recover the underlying structure — namely, individual preferences, the decision process and the resulting intragroup transfers — from the group's aggregate behavior? These are the main questions addressed in what follows.

Our work has a direct relationship with club theory; our models encompass situations in which groups share public consumptions ('local public goods'), or more generally 'confer externalities on each other'

(Scotchmer, 2002, p. 1999). The literature on clubs, however, is mostly concerned with group formation, on the one hand, and the existence of an equilibrium on the other hand — which in turn raises the question of the correct equilibrium concept. In this book, we consider the group as exogenously given, and we assume that the decision process, whatever its specific features, leads to efficient allocations (as we shall discuss below in some detail). Our main interest is in the empirical consequences of these assumptions: do they generate testable predictions on the group's (aggregate) behavior, and to what extent is it possible to recover the group's fundamentals (preferences, decision process) from the sole observation of this behavior (more on this below). In that sense, the two approaches are largely complementary.[2]

Finally, we use, throughout the book, a 'differentiable' perspective; i.e., we consider demand *functions*, which are moreover assumed to be 'smooth' (typically differentiable). An alternative viewpoint relies on a 'revealed preferences' approach, which only assumes the availability of finite sets of price and demand vectors. Although this viewpoint is not presented here, it is largely complementary to our analysis. The interested reader may profitably refer to the work of Cherchye et al. (2007).

Decision process: the collective viewpoint. Any analysis of group behavior faces a basic problem, namely the representation of the decision process adopted by the group. Various paths can be followed at this point. One is to construct a very detailed model, based on specific assumptions — say, a non-cooperative bargaining framework in which agents can make offers in a given order and according to detailed rules, while being characterized by specific fallback options. An obvious drawback of this approach is that, since the predicted outcome depends on

[2] In addition, many technical details differ between the two approaches. For instance, the club literature typically consider individual budget constraints; while this assumption is not incompatible with our setting, our context a priori only requires a budget constraint to be satisfied at the group level (the particular case of individual budget constraints is however considered in Section 5). In clubs, agents typically optimize individually and cannot observe other agents' preferences or endowments, whereas we assume Pareto efficiency. Finally, we do not need specific assumptions on preferences (e.g., transferable utility, or "essential" private goods). For a general presentation of the club literature, see Scotchmer (2002).

the particular rules adopted, empirical applications require a precise knowledge of these rules. We can certainly think of situations in which the rules governing the decision process are indeed publicly known; one may think, for instance, of the allocation of a commodity by an auction, or of the vote of a committee. Most of the time, however, the rules are unobservable; they may actually fail to exist, at least in the formal and explicit sense required by the theory.

In this book, we adopt an alternative, axiomatic perspective. Specifically, we follow the 'collective' approach, initially introduced by Chiappori (1988a,b, 1992) and Browning and Chiappori (1998), and simply assume that the group always reach Pareto efficient decisions. We view efficiency as a natural assumption in many contexts, and as a natural benchmark in all cases. The 'collective' point of view is indeed becoming a standard tool in household economics. Other models, in particular in the literature on firm behavior, are based on cooperative game theory in a symmetric information context, where efficiency is paramount (see for instance the 'insider–outsider' literature, and more generally the models involving bargaining between management and workers or unions). The analysis of intra-group risk sharing, starting with Townsend's seminal paper (1994), provides other interesting examples. Finally, even in the presence of asymmetric information, first best efficiency is a natural benchmark. For instance, a large part of the empirical literature on contract theory tests models involving asymmetric information against the null of symmetric information and first best efficiency (see Chiappori and Salanie 2000 for a recent survey). However, it is important to note that we place no restriction on the form of the decision process beyond efficiency.

Distribution factors. In many situations, the group's decision depends not only on prices, but also on factors that can affect the influence of various members on the decision process. Think, for instance, of the decision process as a bargaining game; since bargaining under symmetric information typically generates efficient outcomes, such a context is indeed a particular case of the collective model. Typically, the outcome of such a game depends on the members' respective bargaining positions. It follows that *any factor of the group environment that may influence the members' respective bargaining strengths will potentially affect the outcome.* Such effects are of course paramount, and their relevance is not restricted to bargaining in any particular sense. In general, group behavior depends not only on preferences and budget constraint, but also on the members' respective 'power'; any variable that changes the powers may have an impact on observed collective behavior.

Variables that affect the members' decision powers within the group are usually called *distribution factors*. In many cases, such variables are readily observable. To take a very basic example, think of the group as a small open economy with private consumption only (in the DMS tradition). Any efficient outcome is an equilibrium; and the particular equilibrium that will prevail depends typically on individual incomes (or endowments). Then initial incomes are distribution factors for the group under consideration. Other examples are provided by the literature on household behavior. In their study of household labor supply, Chiappori et al. (2002) use the state of the marriage market, as proxied by the sex ratio by age, race and state, and the legislation on divorce as particular distribution factors affecting the intrahousehold decision process, hence its outcome (labor supplies in that case). They find, indeed, that any improvement in women's position (e.g., more favorable divorce laws, or excess 'supply' of males on the marriage market) significantly decreases (resp. increases) female (resp. male) labor supply. In a similar context, Rubalcava and Thomas (2000) refer to the generosity of single parent benefits and reach identical conclusions. Thomas et al. (1997), using an Indonesian survey, show that the distribution of wealth by gender at marriage — another candidate distribution factor — has a significant impact on children health in those areas where wealth remains under the contributor's control.[3] Duflo (2003) has derived related conclusions from a careful analysis of a reform of the South African social pension program that extended the benefits to a large, previously not covered black population. She finds that the recipient's gender — still a typical distribution factor — matters for the consequences of the transfers on children's health. Finally, Attanasio and Lechène (2009), studying the conditional cash transfer program 'Progresa' in Mexico,

[3] See also Galasso (1999) for a similar investigation.

which is given to women, show that the consequences over consumption of an increase in income due to Progresa is quite different from any other source of income. Again, they conclude that the gender of the recipient makes all the difference.

Practically, the observation of distribution factors crucially enhances the analytical performance of our models; they allow for more robust tests and more general identification procedures. Distribution factors will therefore play an important role in what follows.

Testability and identifiability. The collective model provides a very flexible tool for analyzing the decisions made by the group. It is compatible with a host of decision processes, from decentralized bargaining to centrally coordinated mechanisms; with a number of structural frameworks, involving private or public consumption, externalities and intragroup production; and with any allocation of powers within the collectivity. While this flexibility is a major advantage of the approach, one may fear it is excessive, in the sense that it deprives the model from any empirical content; i.e., it is not the case that *any* behavior is compatible with (some version of) this general setting? We shall see that, on the contrary, the model, general as it is, still generates *testable implications* on the group's behavior, at least when the size of the group is small enough; remember that from DML, no testable implication can be found for 'large' groups. In a Popperian view, testability is a standard requirement of a scientific approach, hence the importance of this result.

Another requirement is related to what is usually called 'identifiability' of the collective framework. As for any theoretical model, the collective approach relates unobservable, structural parameters (individual preferences, intragroup decision process) with observed, 'reduced-form' behavior — here, an aggregate demand function. Ultimately, our interest is mostly directed at the underlying structure, either because we want to understand the characteristics of the decision process or because we are concerned with welfare issues. An important question, therefore, is whether it is possible to recover that structure from the type of data that is available — i.e., demand behavior.

Testability on the one hand, identifiability on the other hand are the two main problems that this book will analyze.

Identifiability and identification. From a methodological perspective, it may be useful to define more precisely what is meant by 'recovering the underlying structure'. The structure, in our case, is defined by the (strictly convex) preferences of individuals in the group and the decision process. Because of the efficiency assumption, for any particular cardinalization of individual utilities the decision process is fully summarized by the Pareto weights corresponding to the outcome at stake. The structure, thus, consists in a set of individual preferences (with a particular cardinalization) and Pareto weights (with some normalization — e.g., the sum of Pareto weights is taken to be one).

This structure is not observable; what can be recorded is the group's aggregate demand function $\xi(p,y)$. In practice, the 'observation' of $\xi(p,y)$ is a complex process, that entails specific difficulties. For instance, one never observes a (continuous) function, but only a finite number of values on the function's graph. These values are measured with some errors, which raises problems of statistical inference. In some cases, the data are cross-sectional, in the sense that different groups are observed in different situations; specific assumptions have to be made on the nature and the form of (observed and unobserved) heterogeneity between the groups. Even when the same group is observed in different contexts (say, from panel data), other assumptions are needed on the dynamics of the situation, e.g., on the way past behavior influences present choices. All these issues, which lay at the core of what is usually called the *identification* problem, are outside the scope of this paper.

Our interest, here, is in what has been called the *identifiability* problem, which can be defined as follows: when it is the case that the (hypothetically) perfect knowledge of a smooth *demand function* $\xi(p,y)$ uniquely defines the underlying structure within a given class? Formally, for any given structure, the maximization of the (Pareto) weighted sum of utilities generates a unique demand function. This defines a mapping from the set of structures to the set of demand functions. Identifiability obtains if this mapping is *injective*, in the sense that two different structures can never generate the same demand function. In other words, non-identifiability does not result from the econometrician's inability to exactly recover the form of demand functions — say, because only noisy estimates of the parameters can be obtained, or even because the functional form itself (and the stochastic structure added to it) is inadequate — but from deeper structural reasons. The identification problem has, at least to some extent, econometric or statistical answers. For instance, confidence intervals can be computed for the parameters (and become negligible when the sample size grows); the relevance of the functional form can be checked using specification tests; etc. The non-identifiability problem has a different nature: even if a *perfect* fit to *ideal* data was feasible, it would still be impossible to recover the underlying structure from observed behavior.[4]

In the case of *individual* behavior, as analyzed by standard consumer theory, identifiability is an old but crucial result. Indeed, it has been known for several decades that under minimal smoothness conditions,[5] an individual demand function uniquely identifies the underlying preferences. Usual as this property may have become, it remains one of the strongest results in microeconomic theory. It implies, for instance, that assessments about individual well-being can unambiguously be made from the sole observation of demand behavior — a fact that opens the way to all of applied welfare economics. The present work can be seen as an attempt at generalizing this classical identifiability property to efficient groups of arbitrary sizes.

Identifiability is a necessary condition for identification. If different structures are observationally equivalent, there is no hope that observed behavior will help to distinguish among them — only ad hoc functional form restrictions can do that. Since observationally equivalent models may have very different welfare implications, non-identifiability severely limits our ability to formulate reliable normative judgments: any normative recommendation based on a particular structural model is unreliable, since it is ultimately based on the purely arbitrary choice of one underlying structural model among many.

[4] The distinction between identification and identifiability can be traced back to Koopmans's (1949) seminal paper (we thank Martin Browning for suggesting this reference). A difference is that Koopmans defines a 'structure' as 'a combination of a specific set of structural equations and a specific distribution function of the latent variables' — a 'model' being defined as a 'set of structures'. Koopmans clearly distinguishes two types of identification problems, namely those linked with 'statistical inference' and those due to 'identifiablity'.

[5] Essentially, preferences must be lipschitzian (see Mas Colell, 1977).

Note, finally, that identifiability is only a necessary first step for identification (in the standard, econometric sense). Whether an *identifiable* model is econometrically *identified* depends on the stochastic structure representing the various statistical issues (measurement errors, unobserved heterogeneity,...) discussed above. After all, the abundant empirical literature on consumer behavior, while dealing with a model that is always identifiable, has convinced us that identification crucially depends on the nature of available data.

Parametric versus non-parametric identifiability. The identifiability problem may be approached from a parametric or a non-parametric perspective. In the parametric approach, a particular functional form is chosen for the structural model, and a reduced form for the demand function is derived. In such a context, uniqueness or identifiability are *conditional on the functional form*; i.e., they obtain (at best) within a specific and narrow set of candidate functions, namely those compatible with the functional form chosen at the outset. Throughout this paper, our approach, on the contrary, is explicitly *non-parametric*. That is, we try to find conditions that guarantee uniqueness within the general class of smooth, strictly convex preferences and differentiable Pareto weights. One can readily provide examples in which identifiability obtains in a parametric sense, but not in the non-parametric setting (it is then functional form dependent).[6]

In practice, parametric models are often convenient. In particular, we do *not* suggest that parametric estimations should not be used, or even that it should be resorted to with some reluctance. Postulating a specific functional form is a standard, well established and often extremely fruitful methodology. We do however submit that the status of the conclusions drawn from parametric estimations crucially depend on whether or not the underlying model is *non-parametrically identifiable*. If it is, then the reliability of the parametric estimates (and, consequently, of the conclusions drawn from it) is directly related to the quality of the empirical fit, as assessed by standard econometric tests. If the econometrician can convince himself (and the scientific community) that the model provides a pretty faithful representation of

[6] See for instance Blundell et al. 2006.

the real phenomenon, then the same level of trust could in principle be put into the conclusions derived from it. The case is much weaker in the absence of non-parametric identifiability. A good empirical fit is no longer sufficient: by definition, many different structural models, with potentially divergent normative implications, have exactly the same fit (since they generate the same reduced forms), hence are exactly as well supported by the data as the initial one.

Of course, this discussion should not be interpreted too strictly. In the end, identifying assumptions are (almost) always needed. The absence of non-parametric identifiability, thus, should not necessarily be viewed as a major weakness. We believe, however, that it justifies a more cautious interpretation of the estimates. More importantly, we submit, as a basic, methodological rule, that an explicit analysis of non-parametric identifiability is a necessary first step in any consistent empirical strategy — if only to suggest the most adequate identifying assumptions. Applying this approach to collective models is indeed an important outcome of our approach.

Structure of the book and main results. We may now briefly describe the general structure of the book. Section 2 describes the basic framework under consideration; it describes the main concepts and assumptions, and states the questions that will be addressed in the remainder. Section 3, which discusses the first problem, namely the characterization of aggregate demand, which establish several results. First, whenever the number of commodities is strictly larger than the number of group members, the model generates strong testable restrictions on group demand. These restrictions take the form of partial differential equations and inequations (the 'SNR$(H-1)$' conditions) that directly generalize the standard Slutsky conditions of consumer theory. Moreover, these conditions are also sufficient, at least for local integration: for any 'smooth' aggregate demand X satisfying SNR$(H-1)$ and for any regular point p, it is possible to construct a group of H members such that an optimal consumption plan for the group aggregates into X on an open neighborhood of p. Finally, the conditions remain sufficient for local integration even under the additional restrictions that commodities are either all privately or all publicly consumed. A by-product of this result is that the private or public nature of intragroup consumption is not testable from aggregate data on group demand.

Section 4 addresses the second problem, namely identification. We first show that in its most general formulation, the model is not identifiable: any given aggregate demand satisfying SNR($H - 1$) can be derived either from a continuum of models with private consumption only, or from a continuum of models with public consumption only, or actually from a continuum of other models. However, a simple exclusion assumption is in general sufficient to guarantee full, non-parametric identifiability of the welfare-relevant structure. Specifically, the *collective indirect utility* of each member is defined as the utility level that member ultimately reaches for given prices, household income and possibly distribution factors, taking into account the allocation of resources prevailing within the household. If each agent of the group is excluded from consumption of (at least) one commodity, then, in general, the *collective indirect utility* of each member can be recovered (up to some increasing transform), irrespective of the total number of commodities. The result obtains only 'in general' because one can characterize pathological situations in which it does not hold; technically, the demand function must then satisfy a set of partial differential equations (in that sense, these cases are 'non-generic'). Ironically, the most striking example of such a pathology is the widely used unitary setting, in which the group is described as if there was a unique decision maker. While analytically convenient, the unitary representation entails a huge cost, since it precludes the (non-parametric) identification of individual consumption and welfare. One of the main conclusions of this section, therefore, is that in a general sense, *non-unitary models are indispensable for addressing issues related to intrahousehold behavior.*

Sections 5 and 6 are devoted to a particular but widely studied case, that of an exchange economy. The restriction, here, is twofold: each commodity is privately consumed (without externality), so that the group can be analyzed as an exchange economy (efficiency is then a consequence of the welfare theorems); and the intragroup distribution of resources is characterized either by constant individual endowments (the excess demand case, in Shafer and Sonnenschein's 1982 terminology) or constant nominal incomes (the market demand case). Section 5 deals with the case of complete markets. We first consider the so-called 'Sonnenschein problem', which can be stated as follows: in a 'large' economy (i.e., one with more agents than commodities), which properties, if any, characterize aggregate demand? We provide a new and shorter proof for the case of aggregate excess demand, initially solved by Debreu (1974) and Mantel (1974, 1976); we then describe the proof of the (more difficult) market demand case, solved by Chiappori and Ekeland (1999a), before considering in last subsection the case of a 'small' economy. Section 6 extends the previous results to incomplete markets, and generally to constraints on trade.

Throughout this book, the techniques of exterior differential calculus are repeatedly used; they are absolutely crucial to many of the proofs provided. Since these tools may not be familiar to most mathematical economists, we provide a detailed presentation in an Appendix. The Appendix is self-contained, and can be read independently of this book; we believe that its usefulness goes beyond aggregation theory.

2

The Basic Structure

Throughout this book, we consider a group consisting of H members. We first describe individual preferences, then we discuss the modelling of intragroup decision processes. In what follows, the transpose of vector x is denoted x^{T}, and the scalar product of vectors x and y is denoted $x^{\mathrm{T}}y$; i.e., if $x = (x_1, \ldots, x_N)$ and $y = (y_1, \ldots, y_N)$ then:

$$x^{\mathrm{T}}y = \sum_k x_k y_k$$

2.1 Commodities and Preferences

2.1.1 Commodities

Agents may consume N commodities, I of which are privately consumed by each member while the remaining $J = N - I$ are public within the group. Note that, formally, the list of commodities may include leisure; in particular, our model applies to the analysis of labor supply behavior. Moreover, a given, 'physical' commodity may be further indexed by the period or the state of the world (or both) at which it is available. Therefore, our setting extends to intertemporal behavior (savings, investment, human capital accumulation) as well as risk sharing and group decision under uncertainty.

Let x_h^i denote the private consumption of commodity i by group member h, and X^j the group's consumption of public good j. An *allocation* is a $J + HI$-vector $(X, x_1, \ldots, x_H)$, where

$$X = (X^1, \ldots, X^J) \in \mathbb{R}^J \quad \text{and}$$
$$x_h = (x_h^1, \ldots, x_h^I) \in \mathbb{R}^I \text{ for } h = 1, \ldots, H.$$

2.1.2 Utility Functions

General Form. We assume that each person has a utility function over allocations. We denote h's utility function by $U^h(X, x_1, \ldots, x_H)$. This formulation is fully general; it allows the utility of h to depend on the private consumptions of other members in a non-restricted way. This interaction may be the result of altruism (i.e., h cares about other members' well being) or paternalism (h is concerned with her partners' consumptions); it may also reflect other external impacts between consumptions (say, a member's smoking bothers other members by reducing their utility, an intragroup 'externality' in the usual sense). Note, in particular, that other members' consumptions of private goods may impact on h's marginal rate of substitution between her own private and public goods; in other words, we do not impose separability restrictions so far.

The utility functions $U^h, h = 1, \ldots, N$, are assumed continuously differentiable and strictly concave; in some cases, stronger restrictions (e.g., infinite differentiability, *strong concavity*, defined by the fact that the matrix of second derivatives is negative definite everywhere, or *strong quasi-concavity*, defined by the fact that the restriction of this matrix to the subspace orthogonal to the gradient is negative definite) will be required.

Caring. Although quite reasonable, the form just described is sometimes too general — if only because it is difficult to incorporate such preferences into a model in which agents live alone for some part of their life-cycle. Consequently the literature often considers a special case which is known as *caring*. For this we first assume that agent h

has an 'egoistic' subutility function $u^h(X, x_h)$. Then h's preferences are summarized by a utility function over allocations defined by:

$$U^h(X, x_1, \ldots, x_H) = W^h[u^1(X, x_1), \ldots, u^H(X, x_H)] \tag{2.1}$$

In other words, A cares about B's allocation only through the private pleasure that B actually derives from her consumption. Caring rules out externalities and entails weak separability between private consumptions (that is, a member's marginal rates of substitution between her private consumptions do not depend on the private consumptions of other members).

Finally, an extreme case of caring is given by *egoistic* preferences, whereby

$$U^h(X, x_1, \ldots, x_H) = u^h(X, x_h). \tag{2.2}$$

Then h's utility does not depend on the private consumptions or welfares of other members.

Intragroup production. In the most general version of the model, we allow for production within the group. Then the group uses commodities purchased on the market — let $\xi \in \mathbb{R}^M$ denote the corresponding vector — as inputs of a production process described by some *convex* production set Γ; the output $(X, x) \in \mathbb{R}^N$ (where $x = \sum_h x_h$) is consumed within the group. Formally, thus, a plan (ξ, X, x), consisting on an M-vector ξ of market purchase and an N-vector (X, x) of intragroup consumption is technically possible if and only if (with the usual notations):

$$(-\xi, X, x) \in \Gamma$$

An obvious particular case obtains when there is no intragroup production and the group consumes what it purchases; then $M = N$ and Γ is defined by

$$(-\xi, X, x) \in \Gamma \Leftrightarrow -\xi + (X, x) = 0.$$

2.1.3 Aggregate Demand

The group aggregate demand on the market is denoted by the vector $\xi \in \mathbb{R}^M$; the corresponding market prices are $\pi \in \mathbb{R}^M_{++}$. The group has limited resources; specifically, its purchase vector ξ must satisfy a standard market budget constraint of the form

$$\pi^{\mathrm{T}}\xi = y$$

where y denotes the group's total income. Throughout this book, we assume that behavior is zero homogenous in prices and income, in the sense that when the group is faced with prices λp and income λy, where λ is a positive scalar, its demand and consumptions are independent of λ. For many computations, we shall therefore normalize the group's total income to be 1.

With non-trivial intragroup production, a consumption bundle $(X, x_1, \ldots, x_H)$ is *feasible at prices* π *and income* y if there exists a purchase vector ξ such that (i) it is technically possible, i.e., $(-\xi, X, x_1 + \cdots + x_H) \in \Gamma$, and (ii) $\pi^{\mathrm{T}}\xi \leq y$. It is often convenient to introduce a little bit more structure by assuming the existence of a production function f such that

$$(-\xi, X, x) \in \Gamma \Leftrightarrow f(-\xi, X, x) \leq 0$$

where f is strictly increasing, continuously differentiable and strongly convex.

Finally, in the absence of intragroup production, we denote by p the price vector of private goods and P that of public goods, so that $\pi = (P, p)$. A consumption bundle $(X, x_1, \ldots, x_H)$ is then feasible at prices π and income y if it satisfies the usual budget constraint:

$$P^{\mathrm{T}}X + p^{\mathrm{T}}\left(\sum_h x_h\right) \leq y$$

Observability. Throughout this book, we assume that the household demand is observable. In the absence of household production, therefore, we always observe the vector ξ as a function of prices, group income and possibly distribution factors (see below). In some contexts, however, stronger assumptions will be made. Specifically, we say that a commodity is *excluded* from the consumption of a particular member of the group if it is not consumed by this member (i.e., it does not enter this member's utility). We say that a commodity is *exclusive* to member i if it is excluded from the consumption of all members except i. One may think, for instance, of leisure, to the extent that individuals are the only consumers of their own leisure (i.e., assuming away externalities or public consumptions of leisure).

Even when a private commodity is non-exclusive, in the sense that it is consumed by several members of the group, it is sometimes possible to observe each individual consumption of the commodity. For instance, some data sets on household demand independently record male and female clothing expenditures. Such a commodity is said to be *assignable.* The difference between exclusivity and assignability is essentially empirical; a given commodity may be exclusive in some data sets and assignable in others, depending on the list of observables. For instance, if male and female clothing expenditures are independently recorded *and* their respective prices vary independently, clothing is exclusive. On the contrary, if only one price index for 'clothing' is available (or if the prices of male and female clothing are perfectly correlated), then clothing is assignable.

2.2 The Decision Process

We now consider the mechanism that the group uses to decide on what to buy. Different assumptions have been used in the literature. The traditional, and to some extent still standard framework assumes that the group behaves as a single decision maker; i.e., there exists a unique utility that is maximized under budget constraint. A second approach is based on non-cooperative procedures. The key assumption, there, is that no binding agreements can be made between members; individuals maximize their own utility, taking the other members' decisions as given, and the group reaches a non-cooperative Nash equilibrium. In the presence of either externalities or public consumptions, such equilibria will fail to be efficient; i.e., they have the property that an alternative, available decision would have been preferred by *all* members of the group. For a precise description of these approaches, see Browning et al. (forthcoming).

2.2.1 The Collective Approach

Our main focus in this book is the so-called collective approach, initially developed by Chiappori (1988a,b, 1992) and Browning and Chiappori

(1998). The key assumption, here, is that the decision process, whatever its exact nature, *always generates Pareto efficient outcomes.* That is, the decision is ultimately chosen such that no alternative choice would have made *all* group members better off. A formal definition is thus the following:

Axiom 2.1. (efficiency) The outcome of the group decision process is Pareto efficient; the consumption $(x_1,\ldots,x_H,X)$ chosen by the group is such that no other vector $(\bar{x}_1,\ldots,\bar{x}_H,\bar{X})$ feasible at the same prices and incomes could make all members better off, one of them strictly so.

The set of Pareto efficient allocations can be characterized in a number of equivalent ways. First, for any vector (π,y) of prices and income in $\mathbb{R}^{M+1}$, there must exist numbers $\bar{u}_2,\ldots,\bar{u}_H$ and vectors $X,x_1,\ldots,x_H$, which may depend on (π,y), such that $(\xi,X,x_1,\ldots,x_H)$ solves:

$$\begin{gathered}\max_{\xi,X,x_1,\ldots,x_H} U^1(X,x_1,\ldots,x_H) \text{ subject to}\\ U^h(X,x_1,\ldots,x_H) \geq \bar{u}_h,\ h=2,\ldots,H\\ (-\xi,X,x_1+\cdots+x_H)\in\Gamma\\ \pi^{\mathrm{T}}\xi = y\end{gathered} \qquad (P_0)$$

Second, if μ^h denotes the Lagrange multiplier of the hth constraint, the axiom can be restated as follows: there exists $H-1$ scalar functions $\mu^h(\pi,y)\geq 0,\ 2\leq h\leq H$ such that $(\xi,X,x_1,\ldots,x_H)$ solves:

$$\begin{gathered}\max_{X,x_1,\ldots,x_H} \textstyle\sum_h \mu^h U^h(X,x_1,\ldots,x_H) \text{ subject to}\\ (-\xi,X,x_1+\cdots+x_H)\in\Gamma\\ \pi^{\mathrm{T}}\xi = y\end{gathered} \qquad (P_1)$$

where $\mu^1 = 1$.

The equivalence between efficiency and the maximization of a weighted sum of utilities is well known; it requires strict quasi concavity of preferences and strict convexity of the production sets (see Browning et al. (forthcoming) for a detailed discussion). The μ^h are the *Pareto weights* of the program. Clearly, Pareto weights are defined only up to some normalization. In program P_1, the first weight is normalized to be 1. Other normalizations are possible, since the maximization problem does not change when the maximand is multiplied by an arbitrary, non-negative scalar function. For instance, one may define $\bar{\mu}^h = \mu^h/(\sum_r \mu^r)$; then $\sum \bar{\mu}^h = 1$.

A more geometric interpretation is the following. For any given utility functions $U^1,\ldots,U^H$ and any price-income bundle, the budget constraint defines a Pareto set for the group; under the assumptions stated (strictly concave utilities, strictly convex production set) the Pareto set is moreover strictly convex. From the Efficiency Axiom, the final outcome will be located on the frontier of the Pareto set. Under standard smoothness assumptions, this frontier is an $(H-1)$-dimensional manifold, indexed by the vector $\mu = (1,\mu^2,\ldots,\mu^H)$.

An important remark is that the vector μ, normalized for instance by $\sum \mu_h = 1$, *summarizes the decision process*, since it determines the final location of the demand vector on this frontier. In that sense, it describes the distribution of power within the group. If one of the weights, μ^h, is equal to one for every (π, y, z), then the group behaves as though h is the effective dictator. For intermediate values, the group behaves as though each person h has some decision power, and the person's weight μ^h can be seen as an indicator of this power. This 'power' interpretation must be used with some care, since the Pareto coefficient μ^h depends on the particular cardinalization adopted for individual preferences; if U^h is replaced with $G(U^h)$ for some increasing mapping G, the set of Pareto efficient allocation does not change, but the parametrization through the vector μ has to be modified accordingly. It follows that interpersonal comparisons of Pareto weights are meaningless; for instance, the fact that $\mu^h > \mu^r$ does *not* imply that 'h has more power than r'. However, the *variations of* μ^h are significant, in the sense that for any given cardinalization, a policy change that increases μ^h while leaving μ^r constant unambiguously ameliorates the position of h relative to r.

If the μ^h are constant, then Program (P) boils down to the maximization of a unique utility under production and budget constraint. We then get a 'unitary' model, in which the group behaves as if it was a single decision maker. In general, however, the weights μ^h depend on prices π, income y and distribution factors z, since these variables may in principle influence the distribution of 'power' within the group, hence the location of the final choice over the Pareto frontier. The maximand in P is therefore price-dependent; the standard properties of unitary models do not apply in this context. However, the dependence on prices and income has a specific form, which will be exploited in what follows.

Two additional remarks can be made. First, since we postulate throughout the absence of monetary illusion, the μ^h are taken to be zero-homogeneous in (π, y). Second, following Browning and Chiappori (1998), we often add some structure by assuming that the $\mu^h(\pi, y)$ are continuously differentiable for $h = 1, \ldots, H$.

2.2.2 Bargaining Theory and Group Behavior

Some applied models rely on more specific assumptions on group behavior. For instance, many studies postulate that the group's decision is the outcome of some bargaining procedure. In general, members are endowed with *disagreement* or *status quo* utilities, intuitively representing the member's utility if no agreement is reached by the group. Bargaining theory analyzes the determination of the group's decision as a function of the status quo utilities. For instance, when $H = 2$, the axiomatic solution proposed by John Nash can be derived from the maximization of the product $(U^1 - W^1)(U^2 - W^2)$, where W^h denotes the status quo utility of member h. This solution is the only one satisfying invariance to affine transformations, Pareto optimality, independence of irrelevant alternatives and symmetry. Other concepts have been proposed, for instance by Kalai and Smorodinsky, who replace independence of irrelevant alternatives with a monotonicity assumption.

Without entering into the detail of these applications, we can make two remarks. First, most axiomatic approaches to bargaining rely on or imply Pareto efficiency. Therefore, bargaining models are but particular cases of the collective approach described below. Secondly, one can readily see that the bargaining assumption, per se, has no testable content; any solution that is Pareto efficient can be rationalized as the Nash solution of a bargaining model for well chosen status quo utilities. Bargaining model can enrich the structure of collective decision models, but only insofar as restrictive assumption are made on status quo utilities — a point formally developed in Chiappori and Donni (2006)

2.2.3 Distribution Factors

A '*distribution factor*' is defined as a variable that affects neither preferences nor budget constraints, but may have an impact on the decision process within the group. As a typical example, assume that the group income y is the sum of H exogenous, individual components $y_1, \ldots, y_H$. The group faces an aggregate budget constraint of the form $\pi^{\mathrm{T}}\xi = y$, which only depends on its aggregate income y. Still, it is reasonable to allow for the group's decisions to depend on the specific contributions $y_1, \ldots, y_H$ — say, because the influence an individual exerts on the decision process may be expected to be somehow related to the size of her contribution to the group's resources. In that case, the $(H - 1)$ variables $z_1 = y_1/\sum_h y_h, \ldots, z_{H-1} = y_{H-1}/\sum_h y_h$ are considered as distribution factors. More generally, if the decision stems from some bargaining process, then any variable that may affect the status quo utilities is a candidate distribution factor. In practice, several variables can be and have been used as distribution factors in the literature on family decision making: laws governing divorce settlement and alimony payments, generosity of welfare (and in particular single parent) benefits, marriage market conditions, etc.

In what follows, the vector of distribution factors is denoted $z = (z_1, \ldots, z_K)$. In practice, distribution factors matter only (if at all) through their impact on the Pareto weights μ; thus μ is a function of (π, y, z).

2.3 The Case of a Market Economy

A very special case, that has been abundantly studied in the literature, is that of a market economy. Specifically, we assume that:

- there is no intragroup production;
- preferences are egoistic;
- all commodities are privately consumed;
- the decision process is characterized by the fact that each individual has either a constant endowment (in commodities) or a constant monetary income, and maximizes her utility under the budget constraint thus defined.

In other words, there are no interactions between group members except for trades at fixed prices.

Technically, in the case of constant individual endowments, the *aggregate excess demand* of the economy is defined as:

$$\xi(p,\omega_1,\ldots,\omega_H) = \sum_h x_h(p,\omega_h)$$

where $x_h(p,\omega_h)$ solves:

$$\max_{x_h} U^h(x_h) \text{ subject to } p^{\mathrm{T}} x_h = p^{\mathrm{T}} \omega_h$$

Similarly, the *aggregate market demand* of the economy is defined as

$$\xi(p,y_1,\ldots,y_H) = \sum_h x_h(p,y_h)$$

where $x_h(p,y_h)$ solves:

$$\max_{x_h} U^h(x_h) \text{ subject to } p^{\mathrm{T}} x_h = y_h$$

In both cases, the welfare theorems imply that the resulting allocation is Pareto efficient; therefore the market economy just described is a particular case of the collective approach.

2.4 Issues

Throughout the current work, we shall be interested in two specific issues, namely the *characterization* of group behavior and the *identification* of the structural components of the model (preferences, decision process) from the observation of the group's behavior.

2.4.1 Characterization

The characterization problem can be stated as follows. Take a group that satisfy the assumptions made above, and that make Pareto efficient decisions under the constraints defined by its production technology and its budget. What restrictions (if any) on the aggregate demand function characterize the efficient behavior of the group, and how do these restrictions vary with the size of the group? In other words, is it possible to derive conditions that are necessary and sufficient for some demand function to stem from a Pareto efficient decision process within a 'well behaved' group? Technically, consider a demand function $\xi(\pi, y)$ that satisfies two standard conditions, namely homogeneity and adding up (i.e., $\pi^{\mathrm{T}}\xi(\pi, y) = y$ for all π, y), and that is sufficiently 'smooth' in a sense that will be defined later. Are there necessary and sufficient conditions on $\xi(\pi, y)$ that stems from the theoretical structure under consideration — i.e., from the fact that $\xi(\pi, y)$ is a group's Pareto efficient demand?

This question has been abundantly studied in the past for two specific cases. A first (and somewhat obvious) line of work considers groups with only one decision maker — either because it consists of one person only, or because the several individuals composing the group behave as a single decision entity. In this context, two sets of conditions characterize demand. The first is income pooling, which states that only aggregate income (and not each person's contribution) matters for the outcome. Using the concepts introduced above, we can say that, in general, distribution factors should have no effect on demand. The second condition is that the Slutsky matrix of compensated price effects is symmetric and negative. These conditions are necessary and sufficient, in the sense that any demand function that satisfies them can be rationalized as stemming from the maximization of a single utility under budget constraint.

A second line of research has been devoted to 'large' market economies, defined by the fact that the number of consumers is equal to or larger than the number of commodities. The well-known 'Debreu–Mantel–Sonnenschein' literature (see Sonnenschein 1973 and Shafer and Sonnenschein 1982) has shown that no restrictions, besides the standard ones, existed on aggregate demand. Specifically, Debreu (1974) and Mantel (1974) show that any continuous function defined on a compact subset of the positive orthant that satisfies homogeneity and adding up can be decomposed as the aggregate excess demand of a market economy with well chosen preferences and endowments. The case of market demand appeared to be significantly more difficult. Andreu (1982) first established the result for finite data set. Recently, Chiappori and Ekeland proved that any *analytic* function, defined on some open neighborhood of a regular point, that satisfies homogeneity and adding up can be decomposed as the aggregate market demand of an economy with well chosen preferences, even when the distribution of income is exogenously imposed. This last result uses the techniques that will be introduced below.

Until recently, not much was known about the intermediate case of ‘smaller’ groups. In the market economy case, Diewert (1977) and Geanakoplos and Polemarchakis (1980) provide necessary conditions for a given function to be the aggregate excess demand of an economy with less agents than goods; however, the conditions are only shown to be necessary, and their results are specific to the market economy context. In what follows, we will provide a comprehensive characterization of the general case. That is, we provide a set of necessary and sufficient conditions that are valid for any model of group behavior (allowing for externalities, altruism, public goods, production, etc.) that make efficient decisions.

2.4.2 Identification

A standard problem in microeconomics is the discrepancy between what we observe and what we are interested in. Briefly put, we mostly observe behavior, while we are mostly interested in welfare. The problem, therefore, is whether, and to what extent, it is possible to recover the underlying structure of the model, i.e., the structural elements required to make welfare assessments, from the sole knowledge of the group's behavior. As discussed in the introduction, these elements include individual preferences and the decision process, as characterized by the corresponding Pareto weights; and these structural components should ideally be identifiable in a non parametric sense.

While the main issues at stake (which were discussed in the introduction) are well known, the reader should keep in mind a basic methodological remark. In a strict sense, no theory is testable per se. Testing a theory always require a host of additional, *auxiliary* hypotheses ranging from general assumptions on preferences (e.g., intertemporal separability) to technical details related to data collection (e.g., independence of individual observations). Should the test fail, therefore, it may be hard to decide whether the negative finding should be seen as a rejection of the theory or attributed to the failure of such or such particular, auxiliary assumption. This so-called Duhem problem is one of the most debated issues in epistemology. While a precise discussion would be outside the scope of this work, it is nevertheless important to remember an obvious consequence of this point. Namely, when trying to test a theory, one should always try to *restrict as much as possible the auxiliary assumptions required.* In other words, one should primarily aim at testing the *most general* version of the model. In our context, for instance, the goal should be to derive testable implication of the unrestricted framework, that allows for general preferences and interaction, including all types of externalities and public consumptions or production.

When it comes to identification, however, the logic is different. Indeed, generality, in this context, may come at an excessive cost — namely, the type of indeterminacy resulting from the fact that a continuum of different structural models may generate the same aggregate group behavior. In general, identification in economics requires identifying assumptions; the role of the theorist is precisely to investigate which assumption are likely to perform best, in the sense that they provide the desired identifiability property without introducing excessively unrealistic assumptions. Throughout the present work, we will try to follow as closely as possible these methodological guidelines.

3

Characterizing Group Demand: Necessary and Sufficient Conditions

We now analyze the characterization problem. Throughout the section, we consider some vector $\xi \in \mathbb{R}^M$ which represents the group aggregate demand on the market; the corresponding market prices are $\pi \in \mathbb{R}^M_{++}$.

3.1 Necessary Conditions: The Main Result

3.1.1 The SNR($H-1$) Condition

We start with a set of necessary conditions that characterize group demand in the most general framework. In what follows, utilities are of the unrestricted form $U^h(X, x_1, \ldots, x_H)$; we simply assume that U^h is increasing and strongly concave. Also, the intrahousehold production process is defined as above; for expositional simplicity, we assume it takes the form $f(-\xi, X, x) = 0$ where f is strictly increasing, strictly convex and continuously differentiable. Also, we normalize the group income to be 1. Finally, we omit distribution factors for the time being; they will be introduced later on.

Household utility. As discussed above, Pareto efficiency requires that the group demand ξ solves the program (P_1) above. We define the function $\mathbb{U}^H$, from $\mathbb{R}^M \times \mathbb{S}$ to $\mathbb{R}$, where $\mathbb{S}$ denotes the H-dimensional simplex, by

$$\begin{aligned}\mathbb{U}^H(\xi,\mu^1,\dots,\mu^H) &= \max\nolimits_{X,x_1,\dots,x_H} \textstyle\sum_h \mu^h U^h(X,x_1,\dots,x_H) \\ &\text{subject to } f(-\xi,X,x_1+\cdots+x_H) \le 0\end{aligned} \tag{3.1}$$

In words, $\mathbb{U}^H$ denotes the maximum value of the weighted sum $\sum_h \mu^h U^h$ when aggregate group demand is ξ; in that sense, $\mathbb{U}^H$ can be interpreted as the group's utility function. It is crucial to remark that $\mathbb{U}^H$ also depends on the vector of Pareto weights $\mu = (\mu^1,\dots,\mu^H) \in \mathbb{S}$. In particular, $\mathbb{U}^H$ is *not* a standard utility function: since the μ^h are generally price- and income-dependent, so is $\mathbb{U}^H$.

By the Lagrange multiplier rule, there is some $\lambda(\xi,\mu) \ge 0$ such that the solution of problem (3.1) coincides with the solution of the problem:

$$\max_{X,x_1,\dots,x_H}\left[\sum_h \mu^h U^h(X,x_1,\dots,x_H) - \lambda f(-\xi,X,x_1+\cdots+x_H)\right]$$

Lemma 3.1. Assume that f and the U^h are C^3, that the second derivatives $D^2 f$ and $D^2 U^h$ are, respectively, positive definite and negative definite, for $1 \le h \le H$. Assume moreover that maximizer in Problem (3.1) exists for all $\mu^h > 0$ and that the Lagrange multiplier λ does not vanish (so that the the constraint is binding). Then $\mathbb{U}^H$ is C^2 and strictly concave with respect to ξ.

Proof. Under these assumptions, we may write:

$$\mathbb{U}^H(\xi,\mu^1,\dots,\mu^H) = \sum_h \mu^h U^h(\theta) \tag{3.2}$$

where $\theta := (X,x_1,\dots,x_H)$ is the solution of:

$$\sum_h \mu^h DU^h(\theta) = \lambda D_\theta f(-\xi,\theta)$$

$$f(-\xi,\theta) = 0$$

for some $\lambda > 0$. This is a system of $J + HI + 1$ non-linear equations for the $J + HI + 1$ variables $(\bar{X},\bar{x}_1,\dots,\bar{x}_H)$. Because of the strict convexity of f and the strict concavity of the U^h, the maximum is attained at a unique point, so (λ,θ) are well-defined functions of $(\xi,\mu^1,\dots,\mu^H)$.

The derivatives are given by the Inverse Function Theorem, namely from the linearized equations:

$$\sum_h \mu^h D^2_{\theta\theta} U^h(\theta) d\theta - D_\theta f(-\xi,\theta) d\lambda = -\lambda D^2_{\theta\xi} f(-\xi,\theta) d\xi - \sum_h D_\theta U^h(\theta) d\mu^h$$

$$D_\theta f(-\xi,\theta) d\theta = D_\xi f(-\xi,\theta) d\xi$$

The first equation gives:

$$d\theta = \left(\sum_h \mu^h D^2_{\theta\theta} U^h(\theta)\right)^{-1} \times \left[D_\theta f(-\xi,\theta) d\lambda - \lambda D^2_{\theta\xi} f(-\xi,\theta) d\xi - \sum_h D_\theta U^h(\theta) d\mu^h\right] \quad (3.3)$$

Substituting the above equation into the second one yields:

$$D_\theta f(-\xi,\theta) \left(\sum_h \mu^h D^2_{\theta\theta} U^h(\theta)\right)^{-1} \times \left[D_\theta f(-\xi,\theta) d\lambda - \lambda D^2_{\theta\xi} f(-\xi,\theta) d\xi - \sum_h D_\theta U^h(\theta) d\mu^h\right] = D_\xi f(-\xi,\theta) d\xi \quad (3.4)$$

which is of the form $A\,d\lambda = B\,d\xi + C\,d\mu$, with:

$$A = D_\theta f(-\xi,\theta) \left(\sum_h \mu^h D^2_{\theta\theta} U^h(\theta)\right)^{-1} D_\theta f(-\xi,\theta) > 0$$

So we can solve (3.4) for $d\lambda$, and write the result in (3.3), getting the expression of $d\theta$ in terms of $d\xi$ and $d\mu$, that is, the partial derivatives of θ with respect to ξ and the μ^h.

This proves that θ is as smooth as $D_\theta f$ and DU^h, namely C^2, and substituting into (3.2), we find that $\mathbb{U}^H$ is C^2. The derivatives are given by the envelope theorem:

$$D_\xi \mathbb{U}^H(\xi,\mu) = -\lambda D_\xi f(-\xi,\theta)$$

$$D_{\mu^h} \mathbb{U}^H(\xi,\mu) = U^h(\theta(\xi,\mu))$$

The fact that $\mathbb{U}^H$ is strictly concave with respect to ξ follows from a direct argument. Take $\xi_1 \neq \xi_2$, and consider:

$$\xi := \frac{1}{2}\xi_1 + \frac{1}{2}\xi_2$$

We claim that:

$$\mathbb{U}^H(\xi,\mu) > \frac{1}{2}\mathbb{U}^H(\xi_1,\mu) + \frac{1}{2}\mathbb{U}^H(\xi_2,\mu)$$

To see this, note that we must have:

$$f(-\xi_1,\bar{X},\bar{x}_1,\dots,\bar{x}_H)\leq 0$$
$$f(-\xi_2,\tilde{X},\tilde{x}_1,\dots,\tilde{x}_H)\leq 0$$

for suitable bundles $(\bar{X},\bar{x}_1,\dots,\bar{x}_H)$ and $(\tilde{X},\tilde{x}_1,\dots,\tilde{x}_H)$, with:

$$\mathbb{U}^H(\xi_1,\mu) = \sum_h \mu^h U^h(\bar{X},\bar{x}_1,\dots,\bar{x}_H)$$
$$\mathbb{U}^H(\xi_2,\mu) = \sum_h \mu^h U^h(\tilde{X},\tilde{x}_1,\dots,\tilde{x}_H)$$

Setting:

$$(X,x_1,\dots,x_H) := \frac{1}{2}(\bar{X},\bar{x}_1,\dots,\bar{x}_H) + \frac{1}{2}(\tilde{X},\tilde{x}_1,\dots,\tilde{x}_H)$$

we find that $f(X,x_1,\dots,x_H) \leq 0$, since f is convex, and:

$$\begin{aligned}\mathbb{U}^H(\xi,\mu) &\geq \sum_h \mu^h U^h(X,x_1,\dots,x_H)\\ &> \frac{1}{2}\sum_h \mu^h U^h(\bar{X},\bar{x}_1,\dots,\bar{x}_H) + \frac{1}{2}\sum_h \mu^h U^h(\tilde{X},\tilde{x}_1,\dots,\tilde{x}_H)\\ &= \mathbb{U}^H(\xi_1,\mu) + \mathbb{U}^H(\xi_2,\mu)\end{aligned}$$

which proves the claim and concludes the proof of the lemma. □

With this notation, and normalizing income y to be 1, program P_1 becomes:

$$\begin{gathered}\max_\xi \mathbb{U}^H(\xi,\mu) \text{ subject to}\\ \pi^{\mathrm{T}}\xi \leq 1\end{gathered} \qquad (P_1')$$

Let $\tilde{\xi}(\pi,\mu)$ denote the solution to program P_1'. By the Lagrange multiplier rule, there is some $\lambda(\pi,\mu) > 0$ such that this problem can be written in unconstrained form:

$$\max_{\xi}\{\mathbb{U}^H(\xi,\mu) + \lambda(1 - \pi^{\mathrm{T}}\xi)\}$$

Lemma 3.2. Assume the Lagrange multiplier does not vanish. Then $\tilde{\xi}$ is a C^1function of (π,μ)

Proof. The argument is essentially the same as in the preceding Lemma. The function $\tilde{\xi}(\pi,\mu)$ is well-defined, since $\mathbb{U}^H$ is strictly concave with respect to ξ, and solves the non-linear system:

$$D_{\xi}\mathbb{U}^H(\xi,\mu) = \lambda\pi$$
$$\pi^{\mathrm{T}}\xi = 1$$

The derivatives are given by the Inverse Function Theorem, namely from the linearized equations:

$$D^2_{\xi\xi}\mathbb{U}^H(\xi,\mu)d\xi = -D^2_{\xi\mu}\mathbb{U}^H(\xi,\mu)d\mu + \lambda d\pi + \pi d\lambda$$
$$\pi^{\mathrm{T}}d\xi = -\xi^{\mathrm{T}}d\pi$$

As above, we solve the first equation for $d\xi$ and substitute in the second:

$$d\xi = D^2_{\xi\xi}\mathbb{U}^H(\xi,\mu)^{-1}[-D^2_{\xi\mu}\mathbb{U}^H(\xi,\mu)d\mu + \lambda d\pi + \pi d\lambda]$$
$$d\lambda = \frac{-\xi^{\mathrm{T}}d\pi + D^2_{\xi\xi}\mathbb{U}^H(\xi,\mu)^{-1}[D^2_{\xi\mu}\mathbb{U}^H(\xi,\mu)d\mu - \lambda d\pi]}{\pi^{\mathrm{T}}D^2_{\xi\xi}\mathbb{U}^H(\xi,\mu)^{-1}\pi}$$

We find the partial derivatives of λ with respect to π and μ from the second equation, and substitute in the first one to get the partial derivatives of ξ. Since $\mathbb{U}^H$ is C^2, it follows from the Inverse Function Theorem that ξ is C^1. □

A key remark is that for any given value of μ, P_1' boils down to standard utility maximization under budget constraint. As a consequence, the function $\tilde{\xi}(.,\mu)$, which maps $\mathbb{R}^M$ to $\mathbb{R}$, satisfies Slustky symmetry and negativeness for all μ.

Finally, the group aggregate demand ξ is related to the function $\tilde{\xi}$ by:

$$\xi(\pi) = \tilde{\xi}(\pi, \mu(\pi)) \tag{3.5}$$

where $\mu(\pi)$ is the specific vector of Pareto weights characterizing the group's decision process. It follows that:

$$D_\pi \xi = D_\pi \tilde{\xi} + D_\mu \tilde{\xi}.D_\pi \mu^{\mathrm{T}}$$

Slutsky matrix. We now define the Slutsky matrix associated to ξ by

$$S(\pi) = (D_\pi \xi)(I - \pi \xi^{\mathrm{T}})$$

This is the standard definition of a Slutsky matrix, adapted to take into account the normalization $y = 1$.[1] Note, incidentally, that $S(\pi)v = 0$ for all vectors $v \in \mathrm{Span}\{\pi\}$; indeed,

$$S(\pi)\pi = (D_\pi \xi)(\pi - \pi \xi^{\mathrm{T}} \pi) = 0 \text{ since } \xi^{\mathrm{T}} \pi = 1$$

Now, we see that:

$$\begin{aligned} S(\pi) &= (D_\pi \tilde{\xi} + D_\mu \tilde{\xi}.D_\pi \mu^{\mathrm{T}})(I - \pi \xi^{\mathrm{T}}) \\ &= (D_\pi \tilde{\xi})(I - \pi \xi^{\mathrm{T}}) + D_\mu \tilde{\xi}.D_\pi \mu^{\mathrm{T}}(I - \pi \xi^{\mathrm{T}}) \\ &= \Sigma(\pi) + R(\pi) \end{aligned}$$

where

$$\begin{aligned} \Sigma(\pi) &= (D_\pi \tilde{\xi})(I - \pi \xi^{\mathrm{T}}) = (D_\pi \tilde{\xi})(I - \pi \tilde{\xi}^{\mathrm{T}}) \text{ and} \\ R(\pi) &= D_\mu \tilde{\xi}.D_\pi \mu^{\mathrm{T}}(I - \pi \xi^{\mathrm{T}}) \end{aligned}$$

[1] Homogeneity implies by Euler relation that

$$D_\pi \xi \cdot \pi + y D_y \xi = 0$$

The Slustky matrix is defined as

$$S(\pi, y) = D_\pi \xi + D_y \xi \cdot \xi'$$

therefore

$$S(\pi, y) = D_\pi \xi + \left(-\frac{1}{y} D_\pi \xi \cdot \pi \right) \cdot \xi'$$

and for $y = 1$ the result obtains.

$\Sigma(\pi)$ is the Slustky matrix corresponding to the function $\tilde{\xi}(.,\mu)$, as computed at $\mu(\pi)$; as such, it is symmetric, negative semi-definite and satisfies $v^{\mathrm{T}}\Sigma(\pi)v = 0$ for all vectors $v \in \text{Span}\{\pi\}$. Moreover, the rank of $R(\pi)$ cannot exceed that of $(D_\pi\mu)$, which is at most $H - 1$. We can therefore state the basic result from Browning and Chiappori (1998):

Proposition 3.3. (The SNR $(H - 1)$ condition) If the C^1 function $\xi(\pi)$ solves problem (P), then the Slutsky matrix $S(\pi) = (D_\pi\xi)(I - \pi\xi^{\mathrm{T}})$ can be decomposed as:

$$S(\pi) = \Sigma(\pi) + R(\pi) \tag{3.6}$$

where:

- the matrix $\Sigma(\pi)$ is symmetric and satisfies $v^{\mathrm{T}}\Sigma(\pi)v = 0$ for all vectors $v \in \text{Span}\{\pi\}$, $v^{\mathrm{T}}\Sigma(\pi)v < 0$ for all vectors $v \notin \text{Span}\{\pi\}$
- the matrix $R(\pi)$ is of rank at most $H - 1$.

Equivalently, there exists a subspace $\mathcal{E}(\pi)$ of dimension at least $M - H$ such that the restriction of $S(\pi)$ to $\mathcal{E}(\pi)$ is symmetric, definite negative, in the sense that $v^{\mathrm{T}}S(\pi)w = w^{\mathrm{T}}S(\pi)v$ and $v^{\mathrm{T}}S(\pi)v < 0$ for all vectors $v, w \in \mathcal{E}(\pi)$.

Here, SNR$(H - 1)$ stands for 'Symmetric Negative plus Rank $(H - 1)$'. As discussed above, a very appealing property of these conditions is that they stem from the most general version of the collective model; i.e., they do not require much beyond efficiency and differentiability. Also, note that the SNR$(H - 1)$ property nicely generalizes the standard Slutsky symmetry of the unitary model. Indeed, when $H = 1$ (the unitary setting), then $R(\pi)$ is the null matrix and $S(\pi) = \Sigma(\pi)$ is symmetric. In the general case where $H \geq 1$, then $S(\pi)$ needs not be symmetric, and $R(\pi)$ represents the 'deviation from symmetry'; then the rank of this deviation is at most the number of members minus one.

On a more technical side, note that the $(H \times M)$ matrix $D_\pi \mu^{\mathrm{T}}$ $(I - \pi\xi^{\mathrm{T}})$ can be written as:

$$D_\pi \mu^{\mathrm{T}} \cdot (I - \pi\xi^{\mathrm{T}}) = \begin{pmatrix} v_1^{\mathrm{T}} \\ v_2^{\mathrm{T}} \\ \vdots \\ v_H^{\mathrm{T}} \end{pmatrix}$$

where the vectors $v_1, \ldots, v_H \in \mathbb{R}^N$ are linearly dependent.[2] It follows that:

$$R(\pi) = D_\mu \tilde{\xi} \cdot \begin{pmatrix} v_1^{\mathrm{T}} \\ v_2^{\mathrm{T}} \\ \vdots \\ v_H^{\mathrm{T}} \end{pmatrix}$$

$$= \sum_h D_{\mu^h} \tilde{\xi} \cdot v_h^{\mathrm{T}} = \sum_h u_h \cdot v_h^{\mathrm{T}}$$

where

$$u_h = D_{\mu^h} \tilde{\xi}.$$

Also,

$$R(\pi) \cdot \pi = D_\mu \tilde{\xi} \cdot D_\pi \mu^{\mathrm{T}} (I - \pi\xi^{\mathrm{T}}) \cdot \pi = 0$$

since $(I - \pi\xi^{\mathrm{T}}) \cdot \pi = \pi - \pi(\xi^{\mathrm{T}}\pi) = \pi - \pi = 0$. Therefore, $v_h^{\mathrm{T}} \cdot \pi = 0$ for $h = 1, \ldots, H$. By the same token,

$$S(\pi) \cdot \pi = \Sigma(\pi) \cdot \pi = 0$$

Let $\mathcal{E}(\pi)$ denote the subspace orthogonal to $\{\pi, v_1, \ldots, v_H\}$; its dimension is at least $M - H$. Then the space $\mathbb{R}^M$ can be decomposed as:

$$\mathbb{R}^M = \mathrm{Span}\{\pi\} \oplus \mathrm{Span}\{v_1, \ldots, v_H\} \oplus \mathcal{E}(\pi)$$

[2] Obviously, the vectors v_h vary with π, and should be written $v_h(\pi)$. To simplify notations, we shall omit the reference to π whenever it can be done without ambiguity.

and we know that for any two vectors v, w in $\mathcal{E}(\pi)$:

$$v^{\mathrm{T}} S(\pi) w = v^{\mathrm{T}} \Sigma(\pi) w = w^{\mathrm{T}} \Sigma(\pi) v = w^{\mathrm{T}} S(\pi) v$$
$$\text{and} \quad v^{\mathrm{T}} S(\pi) v = v^{\mathrm{T}} \Sigma(\pi) v < 0$$

which shows that the restriction of S to $\mathcal{E}(\pi)$ is symmetric, definite negative, as stated in the last part of Proposition 3.3.

Geometric interpretation. A geometric interpretation of SNR$(H-1)$ is the following. Remember, first, that for any given H-uple of utilities, the budget constraint defines the Pareto frontier as a function of the price-income bundle; then μ determines the location of the final outcome on the frontier. Under smoothness assumptions, the Pareto frontier is actually a manifold of dimension $H-1$. Assume, now, that prices and income are changed. This has two consequences. For one thing, the Pareto frontier will move. Keeping μ constant, this would change demand in a way described by the Σ matrix. Note, however, that this change will *not* violate Slutsky symmetry; that is, it is not different from a traditional, unitary effect. The second effect is that μ will also change; this will introduce an additional move of demand *along* the (new) frontier. This change (as summarized by the R matrix) *does* violate Slutsky symmetry. But moves along an $(H-1)$-dimensional manifold are quite restricted. For instance, the set of price-income bundles that lead to the *same* μ is likely to be quite large in general; indeed, under our smoothness assumption, it is an $(M-H-1)$-dimensional manifold. Considering the linear tangent hyperspace, this means that there is a whole linear manifold of codimension $(H-1)$ such that, if the (infinitesimal) change in prices and income belongs to that hyperplane, then no deviation from Slutsky symmetry can be observed. In other words, *the* SNR$(H-1)$ *condition is a direct consequence of the fact that, in a H-person household, the Pareto frontier is of dimension $H-1$, whatever the number of commodities.*

Non uniqueness. It is important to note that the decomposition SNR$(H-1)$, if it exists, is never unique. To see why, consider the simple case where $H=2$ (then $S(\pi) = \Sigma(\pi) + u \cdot v^{\mathrm{T}}$ for some vectors u and v). Define $\tilde{u} = u + tv$, with $t > 0$. We have that:

$$u \cdot v^{\mathrm{T}} = \tilde{u} \cdot v^{\mathrm{T}} - tv \cdot v^{\mathrm{T}}$$

therefore

$$\begin{aligned} S(\pi) &= \Sigma(\pi) + u \cdot v^{\mathrm{T}} \\ &= [\Sigma(\pi) - tv \cdot v^{\mathrm{T}}] + \tilde{u} \cdot v^{\mathrm{T}} \end{aligned}$$

and the matrix $\Sigma^{\mathrm{T}}(\pi) = \Sigma(\pi) - tv \cdot v^{\mathrm{T}}$ is symmetric, negative and (generically) definite on $[\pi]^{\perp}$. Therefore, we have an alternative decomposition of the form SNR(1).

Inverse demand. An important result is the following: if a demand function $\xi(\pi)$ satisfies SNR$(H-1)$, the inverse demand function, whenever it is defined, also satisfies SNR$(H-1)$. The proof will require the mathematical tools developed in the last section. For the sake of convenience, we provide it immediately:

Proposition 3.4. Let $\xi(\pi)$ be a C^1 function from $\mathbb{R}^M$ to itself, and let $\mathcal{O}$ be an open set on which the Jacobian matrix $D_\pi \xi$ is of full rank; then we can define the inverse function $\pi(\xi)$ on $\xi(\mathcal{O})$. If $\xi(\pi)$ satisfies SNR$(H-1)$ on $\mathcal{O}$, then its inverse $\pi(\xi)$ satisfies SNR$(H-1)$ on $\xi(\mathcal{O})$.

Proof. Consider the differential one-form ω^* and ω, respectively, defined in $\mathcal{O}$ and $\xi(\mathcal{O})$ by:

$$\omega^* = \sum \pi_i(\xi) d\xi^i \text{ and } \omega = \sum \xi^i(\pi) d\pi_i$$

and the associated Jacobian matrices:

$$\Omega = D_\pi \xi \text{ and } \Omega^* = D_\xi \pi$$

By assumption, $\xi(\pi)$ satisfies condition SNR$(H-1)$. Applying Proposition 7.19 in Appendix, we can write:

$$d\omega = \sum_{h=1}^{H-1} \alpha_h \wedge \beta_h + \omega \wedge \gamma$$

and the restriction of Ω to $[\mathrm{Span}\{\omega, \alpha_1, \ldots, \alpha_{H-1}\}]^{\perp}$ is symmetric and negative definite. By Walras Law, we have $\omega + \omega^* = d(\pi^{\mathrm{T}}\xi) = 0$, and hence:

$$d\omega^* = -d\omega = -\sum_{h=1}^{H-1} \alpha_h \wedge \beta_h - \omega \wedge \gamma = -\sum_{h=1}^{H-1} \alpha_h \wedge \beta_h + \omega^* \wedge \gamma \tag{3.7}$$

Since Ω and $-\Omega^*$ are inverse of each other, the restriction of Ω^* to $[\text{Span}\{\omega^*, \alpha_1, \ldots, \alpha_{H-1}\}]^\perp$ must also be symmetric and negative definite. It follows from Proposition 7.19 that $\pi(\xi)$ also satisfies SNR$(H-1)$. □

3.1.2 Testing for SNR$(H - 1)$

How can a property like SNR$(H-1)$ be tested? The basic idea is that a matrix S is SNR$(H-1)$ if and only if the antisymmetric matrix $\mathcal{M} = S - S^{\mathrm{T}}$ is of rank at most $2(H-1)$ (remember that a matrix $\mathcal{M}$ is antisymmetric if $\mathcal{M}^{\mathrm{T}} = -\mathcal{M}$). A more precise statement is the following:

Lemma 3.5. Let S be some SNR$(H-1)$ matrix:

$$S = \Sigma + \sum_{h=1}^{H-1} u_h \cdot v_h^{\mathrm{T}}$$

where the vectors $(u_1, \ldots, u_H)$ are linearly dependent and the vectors $(v_1, \ldots, v_H)$ are linearly dependent. Then the matrix $\mathcal{M} = S - S^{\mathrm{T}}$ is of rank at most $2(H-1)$, and $\text{Im}(\mathcal{M})$ (the subspace spanned by the columns of $\mathcal{M}$) is spanned by the vectors $(u_1, \ldots, u_H, v_1, \ldots, v_H)$.

Therefore, testing for the collective model amounts to testing for the rank of matrix $\mathcal{M} = (S - S^{\mathrm{T}})$. The collective model predicts this rank should be at most $2(H-1)$, while it would be zero in the unitary case. Incidentally, antisymmetry has specific implications for the rank of $\mathcal{M}$. These are given by the following Lemma:

Lemma 3.6. All the non zero eigenvalues of an antisymmetric matrix are imaginary. In particular, an antisymmetric matrix has even rank.

Proof. Let λ be an arbitrary, non zero eigenvalue, $\bar{\lambda}$ its conjugate, and z (resp. $\bar{z}$) the corresponding eigenvectors. Then $\mathcal{M}z = \lambda z$, which implies that $\mathcal{M}\bar{z} = \bar{\lambda}\bar{z}$; we have:

$$\bar{z}^{\mathrm{T}} \mathcal{M} z = \lambda \bar{z}^{\mathrm{T}} z = (\mathcal{M}^{\mathrm{T}} \bar{z})^{\mathrm{T}} z = -\bar{\lambda} \bar{z}^{\mathrm{T}} z$$

Since $\bar{z}^{\mathrm{T}} z = \|z\|^2 \neq 0$, we have that $\bar{\lambda} = -\lambda$ and λ is imaginary. Now, the imaginary roots of a real matrix come by conjugate pairs, so that the number of non-zero eigenvalues is even. □

3.1.3 Distribution Factors

Finally, can these results be extended to distribution factors? The key remark, here, is the following. Condition (3.5) becomes

$$\xi(\pi, z) = \tilde{\xi}(\pi, \mu(\pi, z)) \tag{3.8}$$

therefore

$$D_z \xi = D_\mu \tilde{\xi} \cdot D_z \mu^{\mathrm{T}}$$

A first condition stemming from this relationship is that

$$\mathrm{Rank}(D_z \xi) \leq \mathrm{Rank}(D_\mu \tilde{\xi}) \leq H - 1$$

which is restrictive as soon as the number K of distribution factors is equal to or larger than H. Secondly, assume that a vector $u \in \mathbb{R}^N$ belongs to $\mathrm{Im}(D_z \xi)$; then there exists some $v \in \mathbb{R}^K$ such that $u = D_z \xi \cdot v$. It follows that $u = D_\mu \tilde{\xi} \cdot (D_z \mu^{\mathrm{T}} \cdot v)$, hence u belongs to $\mathrm{Im}(D_\mu \xi)$. Since $\mathrm{Im}(D_\mu \xi) \subset \mathrm{Im}\mathcal{M}$, where $\mathcal{M}$ is the antisymmetric matrix just defined, we conclude that

$$\mathrm{Im}(D_z \xi) \subset \mathrm{Im}\mathcal{M}$$

This property is readily testable, since both $D_z \xi$ and $\mathcal{M}$ are fully determined by the demand function $\xi(\pi)$. Moreover, it implies a linear relationship between the impact of price variations and that of distribution factors on group demand. If a distribution factor matters at all, it must be through its impact on Pareto weights. Since the impact of Pareto weights on demand is already present in the 'deviation' matrix R, there must exist a relationship between the two. As such, this property is very characteristic of the collective approach. Outside the collective framework, it is quite difficult to explain why (and how) the impact on demand of individual incomes or divorce laws, two distribution factors that have been abundantly used in the empirical literature, should be related to price effects.

3.2 Sufficiency: The Basic Mathematical Structure

The conditions SNR($H-1$) has been known to be necessary for sometime.[3] A more difficult question is sufficiency. Take a 'smooth' demand function $\xi(\pi)$ that satisfies homogeneity, adding-up and SNR($H-1$). Can it be constructed as the aggregate demand of a Pareto-efficient group? Formally, thus, the sufficiency problem can be stated as follows: *Is it possible to find (i) functions* $(x_1(\pi),\ldots,x_H(\pi),X(\pi))$, *(ii) increasing, concave utility functions,* $U^1(x_1,\ldots,x_H,X),\ldots,U^H(x_1,\ldots,x_H,X)$, *(iii) a production function* f, *and (iv) a vector function* $\mu(\pi)$ *in the* H*-dimensional simplex, such that* $(\xi(\pi),x_1(\pi),\ldots,x_H(\pi),X(\pi))$ *solves program* (P_1)*?*

In other words, we are looking for an equivalent, in the collective setting, to the *integrability* theorem in the unitary case, whereby Slutsky conditions (with homogeneity and adding up) are sufficient for the existence of a well-behaved utility function generating the demand function under consideration.

We start with a simple methodological point, namely that in order to prove sufficiency, one only has to prove the existence of just *one* set of utility and production functions, however simple. In particular, we may only prove sufficiency in the particular case of no intrahousehold production — i.e., $M=N$ and Γ defined by

$$(-\xi,X,x)\in\Gamma\Leftrightarrow -\xi+(X,x)=0.$$

By the same token, it suffices to prove sufficiency for the set of egoistic preferences of the form $U^h(x_h,X)$.

As it turns out, any demand that is (locally) compatible with the collective approach is compatible with the collective approach without production and with egoistic preferences. Therefore, throughout this section we shall assume away production (therefore assume that $M=N$, so that ξ is a function of $\mathbb{R}^N$ to itself) and only consider egoistic preferences. We shall see below that the conditions SNR($H-1$) are indeed sufficient, although two caveats must be made. First, the proof require some degree of 'smoothness' of the demand; in practice, we shall assume that the function ξ is continuously differentiable. Secondly, the

[3] It was first formulated in Browning and Chiappori (1998).

construction of individual utilities and Pareto weights is only local; i.e., we prove sufficiency in an open neighborhood of any 'regular' point (in a sense that will be precisely defined). The global construction is still an open problem.

Our first task is to describe the basic mathematical structure of the identification problem. We start with introductory examples which show how the structure obtains in two specific but intuitive cases — namely, commodities are either all public or all private. We then address the general setting.

3.2.1 Two Introductory Examples

We now describe the mathematical structure of problem P in more detail. We start with two simple examples that illustrate the main result in an intuitive way. For expository convenience, we disregard distribution factors for the moment.

3.2.1.1 Public goods only

We first consider a version of the model in which no intragroup production takes place (so that $\xi = (X, x)$); we assume, furthermore, that all commodities are publicly consumed (therefore $\xi = X$ and $\pi = P$). Keeping the normalization $y = 1$, program (P_1) above can be written as:

$$\begin{cases} \max_X \sum_h \mu^h(P) U^h(X) \\ \qquad P^{\mathrm{T}} X = 1 \end{cases} \tag{3.9}$$

Let $X^*(P)$ denote its solution. Assuming an interior solution, first order conditions give:

$$\sum_h \mu^h(P) D_X U^h(X) = \lambda(P) \cdot P \tag{3.10}$$

where λ denotes the Lagrange multiplier of the budget constraint; note that λ is a scalar function of P.

Next, we assume that *the Jacobian matrix $D_P X$ is of full rank* on some open set. It follows that the function $X(P)$ is invertible, and we can define the inverse demand function $P(X)$. Then (3.10) becomes:

$$\sum_h \frac{\mu^h(P(X))}{\lambda(P(X))} D_X U^h(X) = P(X)$$

In this equation, the right-hand side is the known (inverse) demand function, while all functions in the left-hand side are unknown — and we want to prove their existence. The specific structure, here, is that the *inverse demand function must be a linear combination of gradients of increasing, concave functions; moreover, the coefficients of the combination must be nonnegative.* Note that when $H = 1$, this equation boils down to a well known result, namely that the inverse demand function stemming from the maximization of a unique utility under budget constraint must be proportional to the gradient of the utility function.

Finally, assume, conversely, that some given, C^1 demand $X(P)$, satisfying $P^{\mathrm{T}} \cdot X(P) = 1$, is regular in the sense just defined in some neighborhood and such that the inverse demand $P(X)$ can be written as

$$P(X) = \sum_h \bar{\mu}^h(X) D_X U^h(X)$$

where the $\bar{\mu}^h$ are positive and the U^h are increasing and strongly concave. Define $\tilde{\mu}^h(P) = \bar{\mu}^h(X(P))$ for $h = 1, \ldots, H$, and consider the program:

$$\begin{cases} \max_X \sum_h^h \tilde{\mu}(P) U^h(X) \\ \qquad P^{\mathrm{T}} X = 1 \end{cases} \tag{3.11}$$

Since the maximand is strongly concave, the first order conditions are sufficient for a global optimum; hence $X(P)$ is the aggregate demand of the group thus defined.

3.2.1.2 Private goods only

The previous argument may seem specific to the public good structure in which it was constructed. As it turns out, the underlying intuition is more general. To see why, let us briefly discuss an alternative polar case in which all commodities are privately consumed and individual utilities belong to the egoistic family. This case that has been repeatedly studied in the literature, starting with Chiappori (1988a,b, 1992). Now the demand function $\xi(\pi)$ is in fact $x(p)$; assuming away intragroup production, the program is therefore:

$$\max_{x_1,\ldots,x_H} \sum_h \mu^h U^h(x_h) \text{ subject to } p^{\mathrm{T}} \left(\sum_h x_h \right) = 1 \tag{3.12}$$

where y has again been normalized to 1. Let $(x_1^*,\ldots,x_H^*)$ denote the solution to this program.

The notion of *sharing rule* provides an equivalent but often more tractable version of this program. It relies on the following result:

Proposition 3.7. There exists H scalar functions $\rho^1,\ldots,\rho^H$ of p, with $\sum_h \rho^h(p) = 1$, such that for any $h = 1,\ldots,H$, x_h^* solves

$$\max_{x_h} U^h(x_h) \text{ subject to } p^{\mathrm{T}} x_h = \rho^h(p) \tag{P_h}$$

Proof. Define $\rho^h = p^{\mathrm{T}} x_h^*$, and assume that x_h^* does not solve (P_h). Then there exists some $\bar{x}_h$ such that $p^{\mathrm{T}} \bar{x}_h = p^{\mathrm{T}} x_h^*$ and $U^h(\bar{x}_h) > U^h(x_h^*)$. But then the allocation $(x_1^*,\ldots,\bar{x}_h,\ldots,x_H^*)$ is feasible and Pareto dominates $(x_1^*,\ldots,x_H^*)$, a contradiction. □

This is just a particular application of the second welfare theorem. Consider the group as a small, convex economy, in which all commodities $1,\ldots,N$ can be produced from a single input, money, according to the linear production technology $p^{\mathrm{T}}(\sum_h x_h) = 1$. Then any Pareto efficient allocation can be decentralized as an equilibrium; moreover, the linear technology requires that the prices within the economy be proportional to market prices p, hence the result.

In other words, when commodities are all private, an efficient allocation can always be seen as stemming from a two stage decision process.[4] At stage 1, members decide on the allocation of total income

[4] Needless to say, we are not assuming that the actual decision process is in two stages. The result simply states that any efficient group behaves *as if* it was following a process of this type.

$y = 1$ between the members; member h receives ρ^h. At stage 2, agents each chose their vector of private consumption subject to their own budget constraint.

The vector $(\rho^1, \ldots, \rho^H)$ is the group's *sharing rule*. In a private good context, the intragroup decision process is fully summarized by the sharing rule; in particular, there is a one-to-one mapping between (normalized) Pareto weights and the sharing rule. This mapping is moreover monotonic in the following sense: if we increase the Pareto weight of member i while keeping the other weights constant (possibly before renormalization), then the new sharing rule allocates more resources to i than the initial one. A nice property of the sharing rule is that it does not depend on the particular cardinalization of individual utilities (it is expressed 'in dollars'). The price to pay for this superior tractability is that sharing rules are less general, being defined for private goods only — although we shall extend the concept to a more general setting below.

Let $W^h(p)$ denote the value of program (P_h): it is called the *collective indirect utility*. It is defined as the utility reached by agent h, taking into account the intragroup decision process. If V^h denote the standard, 'individual' indirect utility of member h, we have that

$$W^h(p) = V^h(p, \rho^h(p)) \tag{3.13}$$

By the envelope theorem applied to program (P_h):

$$D_p W^h = \lambda^h (x_h - D_p \rho^h)$$

where λ^h is the Lagrange multiplier of the budget constraint, i.e., the marginal utility of money of h. Therefore:

$$\sum_h \frac{D_p W^h}{\lambda^h} = \sum_h (x_h - D_p \rho^h)$$

hence

$$\sum_h \frac{D_p W^h}{\lambda^h} = x(p)$$

since $\sum_h \rho^h(p) = 1$ implies $\sum_h D_p \rho^h(p) = 0$.

We can rewrite this equation in a slightly different way. Define $\tilde{W}(p) = -W(p)$; if $\alpha^h = 1/\lambda^h$, we have that:

$$-x(p) = \sum_h \alpha^h D_p^h \tilde{W}^h \tag{3.14}$$

This time, it is the direct group demand function which is equal to a linear combination of gradients. Note that when $H = 1$, this equation boils down to the well known Roy's identity, which states that a demand function stemming from the maximization of a unique utility under budget constraint must be proportional to the gradient of the indirect utility (indeed, when $H = 1$ then $\rho(p) = 1$ and W is the standard indirect utility).

Conversely, assume that some smooth function $x(p)$, satisfying the Walras Law, also satisfies (3.14) in the neighborhood of some $\bar{p}$ for some positive α^h and some strictly decreasing, strongly convex $\tilde{W}^h$ (so that the W^h are strictly increasing and strongly concave). We now show that x can be decomposed as the aggregate demand of a group in which all commodities are privately consumed.

For each h, define a function $\rho^h(p)$ by

$$\rho^h(p) = p^{\mathrm{T}} \cdot [D_p \rho^h - \alpha^h(p) D_p \tilde{W}^h] \tag{3.15}$$

This is a linear first-order partial differential equation for $\rho^h(p)$. Note that the sum $\rho(p) = \sum \rho^h(p)$ satisfies a similar equation:

$$\rho = p^{\mathrm{T}} D_p \rho + p^{\mathrm{T}} x = p^{\mathrm{T}} D_p \rho + 1 \tag{3.16}$$

which has the obvious solution $\rho(p) = 1$.

Equation (3.15) can be solved by the method of characteristics.[5]. It follows that $\rho^h(p)$ can be prescribed arbitrarily on the affine

[5] The method of characteristics will be explained in the last section. In the case at hand, it consists of considering the flow:

$$\frac{dp}{dt} = p$$

in R^N, the solutions of which are given by $p(t) = p(0)e^t$, and to note that the function $\bar{\rho}^h(t) := \rho^h(p(t))$ solves the differential equation

$$\bar{\rho}^h(t) = \frac{d\bar{\rho}^h}{dt}(t) - \alpha_s(p(t))\, p(t)^{\mathrm{T}} \cdot D_p \tilde{W}^h(p(t))$$

hyperplane H defined as the set of p where $\bar{p}^{\mathrm{T}}(p-\bar{p})=0$ (technically speaking, this is a non-characteristic hypersurface, at least in some neighborhood of $\bar{p}$). We choose $\rho^h(p)=1/S$ on H. It follows that $\rho=\sum\rho^h=1$ on H, and since ρ satisfies Equation (3.16), it follows that $\sum\rho^h(p)=1$ everywhere. As a consequence, we have:

$$\sum D_p\rho^h=0$$

Now define:

$$x_h(p)=D_p\rho^h-\alpha^h(p)D_p\tilde{W}^h \tag{3.17}$$

We have:

$$p^{\mathrm{T}}x_h(p)=\rho^h(p)\quad 1\leq h\leq S$$
$$\sum_h x_h(p)=x(p)$$

We now have to show that the $x_h(p)$ solve the consumer's problem. For each h, consider the function:

$$U^h(x)=\min_p\{\tilde{W}^h(p)\mid p^{\mathrm{T}}x\leq\rho^h(p)\} \tag{3.18}$$

Note that, by the envelope theorem, U^h is differentiable and strictly increasing, and $D_xU^h(x_h(p))$ is proportional to p. But Equation (3.17) is the optimality condition for this problem. Since $\tilde{W}^h$ is strongly convex, this condition is sufficient, so that:

$$U^h(x_h(p))=\tilde{W}^h(p) \tag{3.19}$$

Now set:

$$\bar{W}^h(p)=\sup_x\{U^h(x)\mid p^{\mathrm{T}}x\leq\rho^h(p)\} \tag{3.20}$$

We have $\bar{W}^h(p)\geq U^h(x_h(p))=\tilde{W}^h(p)$. On the other hand, for every x such that $p^{\mathrm{T}}x\leq\rho^h(p)$, we have $U^h(x)\leq\tilde{W}^h(p)$. Taking the supremum with respect to all such x, we get $\bar{W}^h(p)\leq\tilde{W}^h(p)$. Finally $\bar{W}^h=\tilde{W}^h$, and Equation (3.20) becomes:

$$\tilde{W}^h(p)=\max_x\{U^h(x)\mid p^{\mathrm{T}}x\leq\rho^h(p)\}=U^h(x_h(p))$$

---

on R. This determines the solution $\bar{\rho}^h(p)$ on each trajectory of the flow. See for instance Bryant et al. (1991) for details.

which tells us that $x_h(p)$ solves the consumer's problem for the utilities $U^h(x)$ and the sharing rule $\rho^h(p)$.

It remains to show that the U^h are quasi-concave, at least in some neighborhood of $\bar{p}$. To do this, pick x_1 and x_2 and a number a such that $U^h(x_1) \geq a$ and $U^h(x_2) \geq a$. We have:

$$U^h\left(\frac{x_1+x_2}{2}\right) = \min_p \left\{ \tilde{W}^h(p) \mid p^{\mathrm{T}}\left(\frac{x_1+x_2}{2}\right) \leq \rho^h(p) \right\}$$

Now, if $(1/2)p^{\mathrm{T}}x_1 + (1/2)p^{\mathrm{T}}x_2 \leq \rho^h(p)$, then we must have $p^{\mathrm{T}}x_i \leq \rho^h(p)$ for $i = 1$ or $i = 2$. Hence:

$$\left\{p \mid p^{\mathrm{T}}\left(\frac{x_1+x_2}{2}\right) \leq \rho^h(p)\right\} \subset \{p \mid p^{\mathrm{T}}x_i \leq \rho^h(p)\} \cup \{p \mid p^{\mathrm{T}}x_2 \leq \rho^h(p)\}$$

$$\begin{aligned} U^h\left(\frac{x_1+x_2}{2}\right) &\geq \min_{i=1,2}\{\tilde{W}^h(p) \mid p^{\mathrm{T}}x_i \leq \rho^h(p)\} \\ &= \min_{i=1,2} U^h(x_i) = a \end{aligned}$$

So the U^h are differentiable and quasi-concave. It is well known that the same preferences can be represented by concave functions, which concludes the proof.

3.2.2 The General Case

In the two polar examples just considered — all goods are privately consumed, and all goods are publicly consumed — the sufficiency problem can thus be reformulated as follows: *when can a given function mapping $\mathbb{R}^N$ to $\mathbb{R}^N$ be written as a linear combination of H gradients of increasing, strongly concave functions from $\mathbb{R}^N$ to $\mathbb{R}$?* Specifically, we have seen that in both cases, this condition was necessary; and that, furthermore, the condition was also sufficient, in the sense that whenever it was fulfilled one could construct a group for which the function at stake was indeed the aggregate demand.

We now show that this gradient structure is in fact general, and that it fully characterizes the collective conditions. As explained above, it is sufficient to consider egoistic preferences without intragroup production. Therefore, omitting again distribution factors, we study the program:

$$\begin{cases} \max_{x_1,\ldots,x_H,X} \sum \mu^h(p,P) U^h(x_h,X) \\ p^{\mathrm{T}}(x_1+\cdots+x_H)+P^{\mathrm{T}}X=1 \end{cases} \tag{P'}$$

Let $x_1(p,P),\ldots,x_H(p,P),X(p,P)$ denote its solution. The household demand function is then $\xi(p,P)=(x(p,P),X(p,P))$ where $x=\sum_h x_h$.

In what follows, we repeatedly use the duality between private and public consumption, a standard tool in public economics. We start with the following, regularity assumption which directly generalizes the assumption made in the public goods case:

Assumption GR (generalized regularity): The Jacobian matrix $D_P X$ is of full rank almost everywhere.

In the neighborhood of a point (p,P) such that $D_P X$ is of full rank, we can consider the following change in variables:

$$\begin{aligned} \psi : \mathbb{R}^N &\to \mathbb{R}^N \\ (p,P) &\to (p,X) \end{aligned} \tag{P_s}$$

The economic motivation for such a change in variables is clear. A basic insight underlying the duality between private and public goods is that, broadly speaking, quantities play for public goods the role of prices for private goods and conversely. Intuitively, in the case of private goods, all agents face the same price but consume different quantities, which add up to the group's demand; with public goods, agents consume the same quantity, but face different (Lindahl) prices, which add up to the market price if the allocation is efficient. This suggest that whenever the direct demand function $x(p)$ is a relevant concept for private consumption, then the inverse demand function $P(X)$ should be used for public goods. The change of variable ψ allows to implement this intuition.

In particular, instead of considering the demand function (x,X) as a function of (p,P), we shall often consider (x,P) as a function of (p,X) (then the public prices P are implicitly determined by the condition that demand for public goods must be equal to X while private prices are equal to p). While these two viewpoints are clearly equivalent (one can switch form the first to the second and back using the change ψ), the computations are much easier (and more natural) in the second setting.

3.2.2.1 Conditional sharing rule

It is convenient, at this point, to introduce the notion of a *conditional sharing rule*, which directly generalizes the sharing rule introduced earlier in the case of private goods. It stems from the following result:

Lemma 3.8. For any given (p, P), let $(\bar{x}_1, \ldots, \bar{x}_H, \bar{X})$ denote a solution to (P'). Define $\rho^h = p^{\mathrm{T}} \bar{x}_h$ for $h = 1, \ldots, H$. Then for $h = 1, \ldots, H$, $\bar{x}_h$ solves

$$\begin{gathered} \max_{x_h} U^h(x_h, X) \\ p^{\mathrm{T}} x_h \leq \rho^h \end{gathered} \tag{P_s}$$

Proof. Assume not, then there exists some $\tilde{x}_h$ such that $p^{\mathrm{T}} \tilde{x}_h \leq \rho^h$ and $U^h(\tilde{x}_h, X) > U^h(\bar{x}_h, X)$. But then the allocation $(\bar{x}_1, \ldots, \tilde{x}_h, \ldots, \bar{x}_H, \bar{X})$ is feasible and Pareto dominates $(\bar{x}_1, \ldots, \bar{x}_H, \bar{X})$, a contradiction. □

In other words, an efficient allocation can again be seen as stemming from a two stage decision process. At stage 1, members decide on the public purchases X, and on the allocation of the remaining income $y - P^{\mathrm{T}} X$ between the members; member h receives ρ^h. At stage 2, agents each chose their vector of private consumption, subject to their own budget constraint and taking the level of public consumption as given. The vector $\rho = (\rho_1, \ldots, \rho_H)$ is the conditional sharing rule; it generalizes the notion of sharing rule developed in collective models with private goods only because it is defined conditionally on the level of public consumption previously chosen. Of course, if all commodities are private $(K = 0)$ then the conditional sharing rule boils down to the previous notion. In all cases, the conditional sharing rules satisfy the budget constraint

$$\sum_h \rho^h = 1 - P^{\mathrm{T}} X. \tag{3.21}$$

As above, the conditional sharing rule can be expressed either as a function of (p, P) or, using the change in variable ψ, as a function of (p, X).[6] In particular, Equation (3.21) implies that

$$\sum_h D_p \rho^h(p, X) = -D_p(P^{\mathrm{T}} X)$$

$$\sum_h D_X \rho^h(p, X) = -D_X(P^{\mathrm{T}} X)$$

We define the conditional indirect utility of member h as the value of program (P_h); hence

$$V^h(p, X, \rho) = \max\{U^h(x_h, X) \text{ subject to } p^{\mathrm{T}} x_h = \rho\} \tag{3.22}$$

which can be interpreted as the utility reached by member h when consuming X and being allocated an amount ρ for her private expenditures. Obviously, V^h is zero homogeneous in (p, ρ).

3.2.2.2 Some duality results

The envelope theorem applied to Equation (3.22) gives:

$$D_p V^h = -\lambda^h x_h$$
$$D_X V^h = D_X U^h$$
$$D_\rho V^h = \lambda^h$$

where λ^h denotes the Lagrange multiplier of the budget constraint (or equivalently the marginal utility of private income for member h) in Equation (3.22). Hence, we have a direct extension of Roy's identity:

$$\frac{D_p V^h}{D_\rho V^h} = -x_h$$

The first stage decision process can then be modelled as:

$$\max_{X,\rho} \sum_h \mu^h V^h(p, X, \rho^h)$$
$$\sum_h \rho^h + P^{\mathrm{T}} X = 1$$

[6] With a slight notational abuse, we use the same notation ρ in both cases. This convention avoids tedious distinctions, in a context in which confusions are easy to avoid.

First order conditions give:

$$\mu^h D_\rho V^h(p, X, \rho^h) = \gamma, \quad h = 1, \ldots, H$$

and

$$\sum_h \mu^h D_X V^h(p, X, \rho^h) = \gamma P$$

where γ denotes the Lagrange multiplier of the constraint. Defining $\gamma^h = \mu^h / \gamma$, we have that

$$\frac{1}{D_\rho V^h(p, X, \rho^h)} = \gamma^h > 0, \quad h = 1, \ldots, H$$

which expresses the fact that individual marginal utilities of private incomes, $D_\rho V^h(p, X, \rho^h)$, are inversely proportional to Pareto weights.

Finally, we have the following conditions:

$$\begin{aligned} \sum_h \gamma^h D_p V^h &= -\sum_h x_h = -x \\ \sum_h \gamma^h D_X V^h &= P \end{aligned} \tag{3.23}$$

Using the change in variable ψ, we see that (x, P), as a function of (p, X), can be decomposed as a linear combination of partial derivatives of V. The nice symmetry of these equations illustrates the duality between private and public consumptions.

3.2.2.3 Collective indirect utility

Following Chiappori (2006), we introduce the following, key definition, which again generalizes that introduced in the private good case:

Definition 3.1. The *collective indirect utility* of agent h is defined by:

$$W^h(p, X) = V^h(p, X, \rho^h(p, X))$$

In other words, W^h denotes the utility level reached by agent h, at prices p and with total income y, in an efficient allocation such that the household demand for public goods is X, taking into account the conditional sharing rule at stake. Note that W^h depends not only on the preferences of agent h (through the conditional indirect utility V^h) but also on the decision process (through the conditional sharing rule ρ^h). Hence W^h summarizes the impact on h of the interactions taking place within the group. As such, it is the main concept required for welfare analysis: *knowing the* W^h *allows to assess the impact of any reform (i.e., any change in prices and incomes) on the welfare of each group member.* Also, note that in the case of public consumption only, W^h is simply equal to the direct utility U^h. Finally, remember that we are using the normalization $y = 1$. Without it, W^h would be a function of (p, X, y) :

$$W^h(p, X, y) = V^h(p, X, \rho^h(p, X, y))$$

where W^h is zero homogeneous in (p, y).

Condition (3.23) can readily be translated in terms of collective indirect utilities: since

$$\frac{D_p W^h}{D_\rho V^h} = \gamma^h D_p W^h = \gamma^h D_p V^h + D_p \rho^h = -x_h + D_p \rho^h$$

$$\frac{D_X W^h}{D_\rho V^h} = \gamma^h D_X W^h = \gamma^h D_X V^h + D_X \rho^h$$

we have that

$$\sum_h \gamma^h D_p W^h - \sum_h D_p \rho^h = -x$$

$$\sum_h \gamma^h D_X W^h - \sum_h D_X \rho^h = P$$

where all functions are expressed as functions of (p, X). From the budget constraint (3.21), letting $A(p, X) = P(p, X)^{\mathrm{T}} \cdot X$ denote the group's total expenditures on public goods, we conclude that:

$$\begin{aligned} \sum_h \gamma^h D_p W^h &= -x - D_p A \\ \sum_h \gamma^h D_X W^h &= P - D_X A \end{aligned} \qquad (3.24)$$

We see that in the general case under consideration, the sufficiency problem can be expressed as follows: *is there a family of differentiable functions $W^h(p,X)$ on $\mathbb{R}^N$, each defined up to some increasing transform, such that the vector*

$$\begin{pmatrix} -x - D_pA \\ P - D_XA \end{pmatrix}$$

can be expressed as a linear combination of the gradients of the W^h?

Decomposing a given function as a linear combination of gradients is an old problem in mathematics, to which much work has been devoted in the first half of the XXth century, particularly by Elie Cartan, who developed exterior differential calculus. We shall use these tools in what follows.

3.3 Sufficiency

3.3.1 The Main Result

In the following, we will solve the sufficiency problem in various contexts. Our main mathematical tool will be the following. Its proof is given in the last section (Corollary 7.4)

Theorem 3.9. Suppose a positive, C^1 function $\xi(\pi)$ satisfies the Walras law $\pi^{\mathrm{T}}\xi(\pi) = 1$ and condition $\mathrm{SR}(H-1)$ in some neighborhood of $\bar{\pi}$:

$$S(\pi) = (D_\pi \xi)(I - \pi\xi^{\mathrm{T}}) = \Sigma(\pi) + \sum_{h=1}^{H-1} a_h(\pi) b_h^{\mathrm{T}}(\pi) \tag{3.25}$$

where $\Sigma(\pi)$ is symmetric, negative, and the vectors $\xi(\pi)$, $a_h(\pi)$ and $b_h(\pi)$ are linearly independent. Then there are positive functions $\lambda_h(\pi)$ and increasing, strongly concave functions $V^h(\pi), 1 \le h \le H$, both defined on some neighborhood $\mathcal{N}$ of $\bar{\pi}$, such that the decomposition:

$$\xi(\pi) = \sum_{h=1}^{H} \lambda_h(\pi) D_\pi V^h(\pi) \tag{3.26}$$

holds true on $\mathcal{N}$.

Corollary 3.1. Suppose a positive, C^1 function $\xi(\pi)$ satisfies Walras law $\pi^{\mathrm{T}}\xi(\pi) = 1$ and condition SNR$(H - 1)$ in some neighborhood of $\bar{\pi}$. Assume, moreover, that the Jacobian matrix $D_\pi\xi$ is of full rank at $\bar{\pi}$. Then there exists H utility functions $U^1(\xi),\ldots,U^H(\xi)$ and H Pareto weights $\mu^1(\pi),\ldots,\mu^H(\pi)$, with $\sum_h \mu^h(\pi) = 1$, such that $\xi(\pi)$ solves Program (3.9) in some neighborhood of $\bar{\xi} = \xi(\bar{\pi})$

Corollary 3.2. Suppose a positive, C^1 function $\xi(\pi)$ satisfies Walras law $\pi^T\xi(\pi) = 1$ and condition SNR$(H - 1)$ in some neighborhood of $\bar{\pi}$. Assume, moreover, that the Jacobian matrix $D_\pi\xi$ is of full rank at $\bar{\pi}$. Then there exists H functions $(\xi_1(\pi),\ldots,\xi_H(\pi))$, where the $\xi_h = (\xi_h^1(\pi),\ldots,\xi_h^M(\pi))$ are such that $\sum_h \xi_h(\pi) = \xi(\pi)$, H utility functions $U^1(\xi_1),\ldots,U^H(\xi_H)$ and H Pareto weights $\mu^1(\pi),\ldots,\mu^H(\pi)$, with $\sum_h \mu^h(\pi) = 1$, such that $(\xi_1(\pi),\ldots,\xi_H(\pi))$ solves Program (3.12) in some neighborhood of $\bar{\xi} = \xi(\bar{\pi})$

In other words, if a function satisfies SNR$(H - 1)$, then it can be derived as the Pareto efficient demand of a group in which all consumptions are public, and also as the Pareto efficient demand of a group in which all consumptions are private. The result is an immediate consequence of Theorem 3.9 because the decomposition into a linear combination of gradients has been shown to be necessary and sufficient in the two particular cases.

These two corollaries provide in practice a sufficiency result: if a given function satisfies SNR$(H - 1)$, then it is possible to construct an H-person collective framework that generates this function as the group's aggregate demand. Moreover, one may impose additional restrictions, such as all commodities being privately (or publicly) consumed without changing the sufficiency conclusion: whenever a demand function is compatible with an H-person collective model, it is compatible with a particular version of this model in which commodities are all private, and also with another version in which consumption is exclusively public.

In particular, we see that the private (or the public) nature of consumption *is not empirically testable from aggregate demand data*: any demand function stemming from a model with, say, private consumption can equivalently be generated from a different model with public consumption only — and, as a matter of fact, from a continuum of alternative models. The same holds for the presence of intrahousehold production: again, it cannot be tested without additional, identifying restrictions. In other words, should a *parametric* version of the collective model be identified (in the standard, econometric sense) without the help of identifying assumptions (such as the exclusivity restrictions that will be introduced below), then one can immediately conclude that the identification comes entirely from the particular functional form at stake. This remark has important implications for welfare analysis; it suggests that one may wish to scrutinize with great care the robustness of the welfare conclusions drawn from a collective model. On a more positive side, it indicates that further investigations are needed on identification issues. Specifically, we need to assess the type of additional restrictions that would allow to exactly pin down the structure (preferences, Pareto weights) that underlies a given group behavior. This will be the main purpose of Section 5.

3.4 Consumer Theory Reconsidered

It is useful to reconsider some standard results of consumer theory from the new perspective just introduced. In addition to providing a fresh interpretation of known properties, this attempt may help understanding the nature of the exterior differential calculus perspective.

We start with the standard utility maximization program:

$$\max_{\xi} U(\xi) \quad \text{subject to } \pi^{\mathrm{T}}\xi = 1 \tag{C}$$

This is the exact equivalent to program (P_1') where the (unique) Pareto weight μ can be normalized to 1; therefore, the household utility $\mathbb{U}^H(\xi,\mu)$ coincides with the consumer's utility $U(\xi)$; as such, it is price independent. As usual, we define the indirect utility function as the value of this program:

$$V(\pi) = \max\{U(\xi) \mid \pi^{\mathrm{T}}\xi = 1\}$$

By the envelope theorem:

$$D_\pi V = \lambda \xi$$

where λ is the Lagrange multiplier of the budget constraint. Therefore:

$$\xi(\pi) = \alpha(\pi) D_\pi V(\pi)$$

where $\alpha(\pi) = 1/\lambda(\pi)$, and the demand function is proportional to a gradient.

In the language of exterior differential calculus, if ω denotes the differential one-form $\sum_i \xi^i(\pi) d\pi_i$, we have that

$$\omega = \alpha dV$$

and from the Darboux theorem, we know that ω must satisfy:

$$\omega \wedge d\omega = 0 \tag{3.27}$$

This condition is exactly equivalent to the Slutsky matrix $S(\pi) = (D_\pi \xi)(I - \pi \xi^{\mathrm{T}})$ being symmetric; a detailed proof is given in the Appendix at the end of this book. Moreover, we want V to be strongly quasi-convex (or actually strongly convex, since we know that a differentiable, strongly quasi convex function always admits a strongly convex cardinal representation). The literature on the convex Darboux Theorem (Chiappori and Ekeland, 1997; Ekeland and Nirenberg, 2002) shows that an additional restriction is needed — namely, the Slutsky matrix must also be negative. Again, detailed calculations can be found in the last section.

Coming back to (C), let us write the first-order conditions:

$$D_\xi U = \lambda \pi$$

On any open set on which the Jacobian matrix $D_\pi \xi$ is of full rank, one may define the inverse demand function $\pi(\xi)$; we see that

$$\pi(\xi) = \tilde{\alpha}(\xi) \cdot D_\xi U(\xi)$$

where $\tilde{\alpha}(\xi) = \alpha(\pi(\xi))$. Therefore, the inverse demand function is proportional to a gradient. Again, the differential one-form $\omega^* = \sum \pi_i(\xi) d\xi^i$ must satisfy:

$$\omega^* \wedge d\omega^* = 0 \tag{3.28}$$

Defining the matrix $T(\xi)$ by

$$T(\xi) = (D_\xi \pi)(I - \xi \pi^{\mathrm{T}})$$

the condition implies that $T(\xi)$ is symmetric; moreover, the concavity requirement for U implies that it is positive.

4

Identification

4.1 Introduction: Opening the 'Black Box'

Broadly speaking, the identification question can be stated as follows: when is it possible to recover the underlying structure — namely, individual preferences, the decision process and the resulting intra-group transfers — from the sole observation of the group's aggregate behavior?

In the (very) particular case where the group consists of only one member, the answer is well known: individual demand uniquely defines the underlying preferences. Not much is known in the case of a larger group. However, recent results in the literature on household behavior suggest that, surprisingly enough, when the group is 'small', the structure can be recovered under reasonably mild assumptions. For instance, in the model of household labor supply proposed by Chiappori (1988a,b, 1992), two individuals privately consume leisure and some Hicksian composite goods. The main conclusion is that the two individual preferences and the decision process can generically be recovered (up to an additive constant) from the two labor supply functions. This result has been empirically applied (among others) by Fortin and Lacroix (1997) and Chiappori et al. (2002), and extended by Chiappori and Ekeland (1997) to household production and by Blundell et al. (2000) to discrete participation decisions. Fong and Zhang (2001) consider a more general model where leisure can be consumed both privately and publicly. Although the two alternative uses are not independently observed, they can in general be identified under a separability restriction, provided that the consumption of another exclusive item (e.g., clothing) is observed.

Altogether, these results suggest that multi-person groups need not remain 'black boxes', the structure of which cannot be investigated without precise information on intragroup decision processes. On the contrary, the group's 'external' behavior, as summarized by its demand function, contains potentially rich information on its structure. In this section, we investigate to what extent, and under which conditions, it is possible to recover much (or all) of the interior structure of the black box without opening it. We first show that in the most general case, there exists a continuum of observationally equivalent models — i.e., a continuum of different structural settings generating identical observable behavior. This negative result implies that additional assumptions are required.

We then provide examples of such assumptions, and show that they are surprisingly mild. Essentially, it is sufficient that each agent in the group be excluded from the consumption of (at least) one commodity. Moreover, when a distribution factor is available, this requirement can be reduced to the existence of an assignable item (i.e., a private item for which individual consumptions are observed). Under these conditions, the structure that is relevant to formulate welfare judgments is non-parametrically identified in general (in a sense that is made clear below), *irrespective of the total number of commodities.* We conclude that even when decision processes or intragroup transfers are not known, much can be learned about them from the sole observation of the group's aggregate behavior. This conclusion generalizes the earlier intuition of Chiappori (1988a,b, 1992); it shows that the results obtained in these early contributions, far from being specific to the particular settings under consideration, were in fact general.[1]

[1] This section is mostly borrowed from the paper 'The Micro Economics of Efficient Group Behavior: Identification', by Chiappori and Ekeland, *Econometrica*, Vol. 77, No. 3 (May, 2009), 763–799.

4.2 Identifiability in the General Setting: A Negative Result

We now state the central mathematical result that underlies most of the following conclusions. It will be applied in various settings. We denote by $\pi = (\pi_1,\ldots,\pi_N)$ the independent variables, and by $\xi(\pi) = (\xi^1(\pi),\ldots,\xi^N(\pi))$ a given vector field. All functions are assumed to be smooth (at least C^2). Also, for expositional convenience, the result is expressed below for a two-person group ($H = 2$); the general case is discussed in the last section.

Lemma 4.1. Suppose four functions $(\bar{W}^1(\pi),\bar{W}^2(\pi),\bar{\lambda}^1(\pi),\bar{\lambda}^2(\pi))$ satisfy:

$$\lambda^1 DW^1 + \lambda^2 DW^2(\pi) = \xi(\pi) \tag{4.1}$$

in some neighborhood Ω_1 of $\bar{\pi}$, and that $D_\pi\bar{W}^1, D_\pi\bar{W}^2, D_\pi(\frac{\bar{\lambda}^1}{\bar{\lambda}^2})$ are linearly independent at $\bar{\pi}$. Then for any other family $(W^1,W^2,\lambda^1,\lambda^2)$ satisfying (4.1) in some neighborhood Ω_2 of $\bar{\pi}$, there exists a neighborhood $\Omega_3 \subset \Omega_1 \cap \Omega_2$ and two continuous functions F and G, defined on some neighborhood of $(\bar{W}^1(\bar{\pi}),\bar{W}^2(\bar{\pi}),\frac{\bar{\lambda}^1}{\bar{\lambda}^2}(\bar{\pi}))$ in $\mathbb{R}^3$, such that, for all $\pi \in \Omega_3$:

$$W^1(\pi) = F\left[\bar{W}^1(\pi),\bar{W}^2(\pi),\frac{\bar{\lambda}^1}{\bar{\lambda}^2}(\pi)\right] \tag{4.2}$$

$$W^2(\pi) = G\left[\bar{W}^1(\pi),\bar{W}^2(\pi),\frac{\bar{\lambda}^1}{\bar{\lambda}^2}(\pi)\right] \tag{4.3}$$

The functions $F(t_1,t_2,t_3)$ and $G(t_1,t_2,t_3)$ must moreover satisfy the partial differential equation:

$$\frac{\partial G}{\partial t_1}\frac{\partial F}{\partial t_3} - \frac{\partial G}{\partial t_3}\frac{\partial F}{\partial t_1} = t_3\left(\frac{\partial G}{\partial t_2}\frac{\partial F}{\partial t_3} - \frac{\partial G}{\partial t_3}\frac{\partial F}{\partial t_2}\right). \tag{4.4}$$

Finally, λ^1 and λ^2 are completely determined by the choice of F and G.

Proof. This is Proposition 7.17 in the last Section. □

Lemma 4.1 provides two conclusions. One is that whenever a given function can be decomposed as a linear combination of two gradients, this can be done in a continuum of different ways. Secondly, one can exactly characterize the set of such solutions. Specifically, the decomposition is identified up to a pair of functions of three variables; moreover, these functions are linked by a partial differential equation.

An immediate implication is the following:

Corollary 4.1. In the collective model, the collective indirect utilities of the members are *not* uniquely determined by the knowledge of household demand.

To get a better intuition of this result, it is useful to consider the particular case in which all goods are public. Remember that in that case the collective indirect utility of a member is simply the person's direct utility. Now, let $(\bar{U}^1, \bar{U}^2)$ be a particular solution; the inverse demand $P(X)$ can be written as a linear combination of the gradients of $(\bar{U}^1, \bar{U}^2)$ — say:

$$\bar{\lambda}^1 D_X \bar{U}^1 + \bar{\lambda}^2 D_X \bar{U}^2 = P(X)$$

Define

$$U^1(X) = F(\bar{U}^1(X), \bar{U}^2(X))$$
$$U^2(X) = G(\bar{U}^1(X), \bar{U}^2(X))$$

where F and G are arbitrary, increasing functions. Clearly, a linear combination of the gradients of U^1 and U^2 must be a linear combination of the gradients of $\bar{U}^1$ and $\bar{U}^2$. The economic intuition is that any allocation X which is Pareto efficient for (U^1, U^2) must also be Pareto efficient for $(\bar{U}^1, \bar{U}^2)$ (otherwise it would be possible to increase both $\bar{U}^1$ and $\bar{U}^2$, but this would increase U^1 and U^2 as well, a contradiction). This gives a first intuition why the Pareto efficiency assumption is not sufficient to distinguish between the two solutions: if a demand function can be collectively rationalized by a couple with utilities (U^1, U^2) then it can also be collectively rationalized by a couple with utilities $(\bar{U}^1, \bar{U}^2)$.

Interestingly enough, this is not the only degree of indeterminacy. To get a different example, set $\bar{\theta}(X) = (\bar{\lambda}^1(X)/\bar{\lambda}^2(X))$, and define:

$$U^1(X) = \bar{U}^1(X) + \bar{U}^2(X) + \bar{\theta}(X)$$
$$U^2(X) = -\bar{U}^1(X) + \log(1 - \bar{\theta}(X))$$

Note that this construct has the form (4.2) and (4.3), and that the corresponding F and G functions satisfy (4.4). Now, $D_X U^1 = D_X \bar{U}^1 + D_X \bar{U}^2 + D_X \bar{\theta}$ and $D_X U^2 = -D_X \bar{U}^1 - (D_X \bar{\theta})/(1-\bar{\theta})$. Therefore:

$$D_X U^1 + (1-\bar{\theta}) D_X U^2 = \bar{\theta} D_X \bar{U}^1 + D_X \bar{U}^2$$

and finally

$$\bar{\lambda}^2 D_X U^1 + (\bar{\lambda}^2 - \bar{\lambda}^1) D_X U^2 = \bar{\lambda}^1 D_X \bar{U}^1 + \bar{\lambda}^2 D_X \bar{U}^2 = P(X)$$

We conclude that the demand function can also be collectively rationalized by a couple with utilities (U^1, U^2).

4.3 Identifiability Under Exclusion

The previous section concludes that identifiability does not obtain in the general version of the collective model. The next step is to find specific, additional assumptions that guarantee identifiability. We now show that a simple exclusion condition is sufficient in general.

4.3.1 The Main Result

In what follows, we assume that $N \geq 4$. Again, suppose four functions $(\bar{W}^1(\pi), \bar{W}^2(\pi), \bar{\lambda}^1(\pi), \bar{\lambda}^2(\pi))$ satisfy Equation (4.1) in some neighborhood Ω_1 of $\bar{\pi}$. We shall say that this solution is *regular* if $D_\pi \bar{W}^1, D_\pi \bar{W}^2$ and $D_\pi \bar{\theta}$ are linearly independent at $\bar{\pi}$, and

$$\frac{\partial \bar{W}^2}{\partial \pi_1}(\pi) \neq 0 \text{ and } \bar{D}_{a,b,c,d}(\bar{\pi}) \neq 0 \quad \text{for some } a,b,c,d \in \{1,\ldots,N\} \tag{4.5}$$

where:

$$\bar{\theta}(\pi) = \frac{\bar{\lambda}^1(\pi)}{\bar{\lambda}^2(\pi)}, \quad \bar{\Phi}(\pi) = \frac{\partial \bar{\theta}}{\partial \pi_1}(\pi) \left[\frac{\partial \bar{W}^2}{\partial \pi_1}(\pi)\right]^{-1} \tag{4.6}$$

$$\bar{D}_{a,b,c,d} = \begin{vmatrix} \frac{\partial \bar{\Phi}}{\partial \pi_a} & \frac{\partial \bar{W}^1}{\partial \pi_a} & \frac{\partial \bar{W}^2}{\partial \pi_a} & \frac{\partial \bar{\theta}}{\partial \pi_a} \\ \frac{\partial \bar{\Phi}}{\partial \pi_b} & \frac{\partial \bar{W}^1}{\partial \pi_b} & \frac{\partial \bar{W}^2}{\partial \pi_b} & \frac{\partial \bar{\theta}}{\partial \pi_b} \\ \frac{\partial \bar{\Phi}}{\partial \pi_c} & \frac{\partial \bar{W}^1}{\partial \pi_c} & \frac{\partial \bar{W}^2}{\partial \pi_c} & \frac{\partial \bar{\theta}}{\partial \pi_c} \\ \frac{\partial \bar{\Phi}}{\partial \pi_d} & \frac{\partial \bar{W}^1}{\partial \pi_d} & \frac{\partial \bar{W}^2}{\partial \pi_d} & \frac{\partial \bar{\theta}}{\partial \pi_d} \end{vmatrix} \tag{4.7}$$

Note that if relations (4.5), (4.6) and (4.7) hold at $\bar{\pi}$, they will hold in a neighborhood of $\bar{\pi}$ as well. Note also that in a practical situation, there is no reason to expect that the functions $\bar{W}^1$, $\bar{W}^2$ and $\bar{\theta} = \bar{\lambda}^1/\bar{\lambda}^2$ would satisfy these equations, and if they do, a slight perturbation of the model would ensure that they do not.

We shall say that π_1 is *excluded from* $\bar{W}^1$ in Ω if:

$$\frac{\partial \bar{W}^1}{\partial \pi_1}(\pi) = 0, \quad \forall \pi \in \Omega \tag{4.8}$$

We now show that exclusion is sufficient to guarantee identifiability for generic models. Note, first, that the result is obvious if the number of commodities is exactly 2 — since individual consumptions are perfectly observed in that case. Also, the case $N = 3$ has been already solved by Chiappori (1992) for private goods and Blundell et al. (2006) for public goods. We are thus left with the general case $N \geq 4$. The main result is the following:

Proposition 4.2. Let $N \geq 4$, assume that Equation (4.1) has a regular solution $(\bar{W}^1, \bar{W}^2, \bar{\lambda}^1, \bar{\lambda}^2)$ in some neighborhood Ω_1 of $\bar{\pi}$, where $\pi_1$is excluded from $\bar{W}^1$. Let $(W^1, W^2, \lambda^1, \lambda^2)$ be another solution on Ω_1, in which π_1 is *excluded from* $\bar{W}^1$. Then there exist a function F and a neighborhood $\Omega_2 \subset \Omega_1$ of $\bar{\pi}$ such that $W_1 = F(\bar{W}_1)$ on Ω_2, i.e., W_1 is ordinally identified.

Proof. >From Lemma 7.17, we know that there is some neighborhood $\Omega_2 \subset \Omega_1$ and some function F such that:

$$W^1 = F(\bar{W}^1, \bar{W}^2, \bar{\theta}) \quad \text{on } \Omega_2$$

Without loss of generality, it can be assumed that Equations (4.5)–(4.7) hold for all $\pi \in \Omega_2$. From the exclusion condition for W^1 and $\bar{W}^1$, we derive, for all $\pi \in \Omega_2$:

$$0 = \frac{\partial W^1}{\partial \pi_1}(\pi) = F_2(\bar{W}^1, \bar{W}^2, \bar{\theta}) \frac{\partial \bar{W}^2}{\partial \pi_1} + F_3(\bar{W}^1, \bar{W}^2, \bar{\theta}) \frac{\partial \bar{\theta}}{\partial \pi_1} \tag{4.9}$$

Suppose $F_3(\bar{W}^1(\pi), \bar{W}^2(\pi), \bar{\theta}(\pi)) \neq 0$ for some $\pi \in \Omega_2$. Equation (4.9) then implies that:

$$\bar{\Phi}(\pi) = \frac{\partial \bar{\theta}}{\partial \pi_1}(\pi) \left[\frac{\partial \bar{W}^2}{\partial \pi_1}(\pi) \right]^{-1} = -\frac{F_2(\bar{W}^1, \bar{W}^2, \bar{\theta})}{F_3(\bar{W}^1, \bar{W}^2, \bar{\theta})}$$

in some neighborhood $\Omega_3 \subset \Omega_2$ of π. So $\bar{\Phi}$ is a function of $(\bar{W}^1, \bar{W}^2, \bar{\theta})$, and its gradient must be a linear combination of the gradients of $\bar{W}^1, \bar{W}^2$ and $\bar{\theta}$. For $N \geq 4$, this translates into $\bar{D}_{a,b,c,d}(\bar{\pi}) = 0$ for all $a, b, c, d \in \{1, \ldots, N\}$. But this contradicts the fact that relation (4.5) holds for all π in Ω_2.

So we must have $F_3(\bar{W}^1(\pi), \bar{W}^2(\pi), \bar{\theta}(\pi)) = 0$ for all $\pi \in \Omega_2$. Then Equation (4.9) becomes:

$$0 = F_2(\bar{W}^1(\pi), \bar{W}^2(\pi), \bar{\theta}(\pi)) \frac{\partial \bar{W}^2}{\partial \pi_1}(\pi)$$

which in turn implies $F_2(\bar{W}^1(\pi), \bar{W}^2(\pi), \bar{\theta}(\pi)) = 0$. We are left with $W^1(\pi) = F[\bar{W}^1(\pi)]$, as announced. □

Proposition 4.2 states that, broadly speaking, a simple exclusion condition is sufficient to obtain identifiability. Note that the result is specific to one of the functions: if W^1 does not depend on π_1, then W^1 is ordinally identifiable, irrespective of W^2 (which may not be).

4.3.2 Generalized Separability

The previous result has an important extension, that generalizes the notion of separability. Let $\rho: \Omega_1 \to \mathbb{R}^N$ be given, where Ω_1 is a neighborhood of $\bar{\pi}$ in $\mathbb{R}^N$, and assume that

$$\frac{\partial \rho}{\partial \pi_N}(\pi) \neq 0 \quad \forall \pi \in \Omega_1 \tag{4.10}$$

Suppose four functions $(\bar{W}^1(\pi), \bar{W}^2(\pi), \bar{\lambda}^1(\pi), \bar{\lambda}^2(\pi))$ satisfy Equation (4.1) in some neighborhood $\Omega_2 \subset \Omega_1$ of $\bar{\pi}$. We shall say that this solution is *separably regular* if $(\partial \bar{W}^1 / \partial \pi_N)$ does not vanish on Ω_1, if $D_\pi \bar{W}^1(\bar{\pi})$, $D_\pi \bar{W}^2(\bar{\pi})$, and $D_\pi \bar{\theta}(\bar{\pi})$ are linearly independent, and if

$$\frac{\partial \bar{W}^2}{\partial \pi_1} \left[\frac{\partial \bar{W}^2}{\partial \pi_N} \right]^{-1}, \quad \frac{\partial \bar{\theta}}{\partial \pi_1} \left[\frac{\partial \bar{\theta}}{\partial \pi_N} \right]^{-1}, \quad \frac{\partial \rho}{\partial \pi_1} \left[\frac{\partial \rho}{\partial \pi_N} \right]^{-1} \tag{4.11}$$

are pairwise distinct on Ω_1, with $\bar{\theta} = \bar{\lambda}^1 / \bar{\lambda}^2$, as above.

We now introduce a generalized separability conditions, which states that all solutions depend on two particular variables, say π_1 and π_N, only through the same function ρ. This is a well-known consequence of separability in standard consumer theory (when a set of commodities is separable, their demand depends on the other prices only through an income effect), which explains the expression 'generalized separability'.

Technically, let ρ be a given, smooth function. We shall say that $\bar{W}^1$ is *separable for* ρ if:

$$\frac{\partial \rho}{\partial \pi_N}(\pi)\frac{\partial \bar{W}^1}{\partial \pi_1}(\pi) = \frac{\partial \bar{W}^1}{\partial \pi_N}(\pi)\frac{\partial \rho}{\partial \pi_1}(\pi) \tag{4.12}$$

Corollary 4.2. Let $N \geq 4$. Assume that $(\bar{W}^1, \bar{W}^2, \bar{\lambda}^1, \bar{\lambda}^2)$ is a separably regular solution of equation (4.1) on Ω_2 and that $\bar{W}^1$ is separable for ρ. Let $(W^1, W^2, \lambda^1, \lambda^2)$ be another solution on Ω_2, with W^1 separable for the same ρ. Then there exist a function F and a neighborhood $\Omega_3 \subset \Omega_2$ of $\bar{\pi}$ such that $W_1 = F(\bar{W}_1)$ on Ω_3, i.e., W_1 is ordinally identified.

Proof. We claim that W^1 can be written under the form:

$$W^1(\pi) = K^1[\pi_2, \ldots, \pi_{N-1}, \rho(\pi)] \tag{4.13}$$

Indeed, the map:

$$(\pi_1, \pi_2, \ldots, \pi_N) \to (\pi_1, \pi_2, \ldots, \pi_{N-1}, \rho(\pi)) \tag{4.14}$$

is invertible in a neighborhood Ω_3 of $\bar{\pi}$ by condition (4.10). So W^1 can be written as:

$$W^1(\pi) = K^1[\pi_1, \pi_2, \ldots, \pi_{N-1}, \rho(\pi)]$$

Differentiating, we get:

$$\frac{\partial W^1}{\partial \pi_1} = \frac{\partial K^1}{\partial \pi_1} + \frac{\partial K^1}{\partial \rho}\frac{\partial \rho}{\partial \pi_1}$$

$$\frac{\partial W^1}{\partial \pi_N} = \frac{\partial K^1}{\partial \rho}\frac{\partial \rho}{\partial \pi_N}$$

$$\frac{\partial W^1}{\partial \pi_1}\left[\frac{\partial W^1}{\partial \pi_N}\right]^{-1} = \frac{\partial K^1}{\partial \pi_1}\left[\frac{\partial K^1}{\partial \rho}\frac{\partial \rho}{\partial \pi_N}\right]^{-1} + \frac{\partial \rho}{\partial \pi_1}\left[\frac{\partial \rho}{\partial \pi_N}\right]^{-1}$$

Condition (4.12) then implies that $\partial K^1/\partial\pi_1 = 0$ for all π, and (4.13) is proved. Taking $(\pi_1,\pi_2,\ldots,\pi_{N-1},\rho)$ as local coordinates, we find that $W^1 = K^1(\pi_2,\ldots,\pi_{N-1},\rho)$ does not depend on the first coordinate, and proposition 4.2 applies. □

Corollary 4.2 shows that generalized separability is but a particular form of exclusion restriction, so that the general identifiability result applies in that case as well. As it turns out, while Proposition 4.2 directly relates to public goods, Corollary 4.2 is easier to use in a private goods context.

Finally, note that if either the exclusion or the generalized separability properties apply to both members, then both W^1 and W^2 are ordinally identifiable. Then for any cardinalization of W^1 and W^2, the coefficients λ^i are identifiable as well.

4.3.3 The Genericity of 'Regular' Solutions

Before discussing the economic interpretation of the previous results, a remark is in order. In Proposition 4.2 and Corollary 4.2, identifiability only obtains for 'regular' solutions. Technically, what Proposition 4.2 shows is that identifiability obtains unless the structural functions $\bar{W}^1, \bar{W}^2$ and $\bar{\theta}$ satisfy a set of partial differential equations that can be explicitly derived. It is thus important to understand the exact scope of these partial differential equations, and particularly to discuss examples in which they are satisfied everywhere.

An obvious case in which the equations are always fulfilled obtains when $\bar{\theta}$ is constant: $\bar{\Phi}$ is then identically null, and so are the determinants $\bar{D}_{a,b,c,d}$ in condition (4.7). This result is by no means surprising. Indeed, if $\bar{\theta}$ is a constant (say k), then $\bar{\lambda}^2(\pi) = k\bar{\lambda}^1(\pi)$ for all π, and Equation (4.1) becomes:

$$\begin{aligned}\xi(\pi) &= \lambda^1(\pi)[D_\pi W^1(\pi) + kD_\pi W^2(\pi)] \\ &= \lambda^1(\pi)D_\pi[W^1(\pi) + kW^2(\pi)]\end{aligned}$$

In that case, the function ξ is in fact proportional to a single gradient; economically, the group behaves as a single consumer with an indirect utility equal to $W^1(\pi) + kW^2(\pi)$. The non-identifiability conclusion is indeed expected in that case: clearly, there exists a continuum of pairs $(W^1(\pi), W^2(\pi))$ that add up to the same weighted sum $W^1(\pi) + kW^2(\pi)$. Note that exclusivity does not help here, unless it applies to all variables. If there exists one variable, say N, that enter both utilities, then if $(W^1(\pi), W^2(\pi))$ is a solution, so is $(W^1(\pi) + kf(\pi_N), W^2(\pi) - f(\pi_N))$ for any arbitrary function f.

We conclude that when a group behaves as a single consumer, then individual preferences are not identifiable. Ironically, a large fraction of the literature devoted to household behavior tends to assume a unitary setting, in which the group is described as a unique decision maker. Our conclusions show that this approach, while analytically convenient, entails a huge cost, since it precludes the (non-parametric) identification of individual consumption and welfare. In a general sense, *non-unitary models are indispensable for addressing issues related to intrahousehold allocation.*[2]

Finally, except for these particular cases, the identifiability result is quite robust; technically, a 'generic' demand cannot satisfy a predefined PDE. It is easy to check, for instance, that whenever a particular solution $(\bar{W}^1, \bar{W}^2, \bar{\theta})$ is non-regular, so that the equality obtains in conditions (4.5), non-regularity is not robust to slight perturbations of either preferences or weights. Consider, for instance, linear versions of all functions:

$$\bar{\lambda}^1(\pi) = \sum_i \lambda_i^1 \pi_i, \bar{\lambda}^2(\pi) = \sum_i \lambda_i^2 \pi_i$$

so that:

$$\bar{\theta}(\pi) = \frac{\sum_i \lambda_i^1 \pi_i}{\sum_i \lambda_i^2 \pi_i}, \quad \bar{W}^1(\pi) = \sum_i w_i^1 \pi_i, \bar{W}^2(\pi) = \sum_i w_i^2 \pi_i$$

Assume that the conditions (4.8) are satisfied:

$$w_1^1 = 0, w_1^2 \neq 0, \sum_i (\lambda_1^1 \lambda_i^2 - \lambda_1^2 \lambda_i^1) \pi_i \neq 0$$

[2] More generally, Proposition 4.2 does not apply if $\partial\bar{\theta}(\pi)/\partial\pi_1 = 0$; again, Φ is then the null function. It is thus important to check that this condition is satisfied. For empirical applications, however, we shall see that it is likely to hold unless $\bar{\theta}$ is constant.

(note that the last inequality is satisfied whenever one at least of the $(\lambda_1^1\lambda_i^2 - \lambda_1^2\lambda_i^1)$ is non-zero — i.e., whenever λ^1 and λ^2 are not proportional).

Then

$$\bar{\Phi}(\pi) = \frac{\partial\bar{\theta}/\partial\pi_1}{\partial\bar{W}^2/\partial\pi_1} = \frac{\sum_i(\lambda_1^1\lambda_i^2 - \lambda_1^2\lambda_i^1)\pi_i}{w_1^2(\sum_i\lambda_i^2\pi_i)^2}$$

therefore

$$\bar{D}_{a,b,c,d} = \begin{vmatrix} \frac{(\lambda_1^1\lambda_a^2-\lambda_1^2\lambda_a^1)(\sum_i\lambda_i^2\pi_i)-2\lambda_a^2(\sum_i(\lambda_1^1\lambda_i^2-\lambda_1^2\lambda_i^1)\pi_i)}{w_1^2(\sum_i\lambda_i^2\pi_i)^3} & w_a^1 & w_a^2 & \frac{\sum_i(\lambda_a^1\lambda_i^2-\lambda_a^2\lambda_i^1)\pi_i}{(\sum_i\lambda_i^2\pi_i)^2} \\ \frac{(\lambda_1^1\lambda_b^2-\lambda_1^2\lambda_b^1)(\sum_i\lambda_i^2\pi_i)-2\lambda_b^2(\sum_i(\lambda_1^1\lambda_i^2-\lambda_1^2\lambda_i^1)\pi_i)}{w_1^2(\sum_i\lambda_i^2\pi_i)^3} & w_b^1 & w_b^2 & \frac{\sum_i(\lambda_b^1\lambda_i^2-\lambda_b^2\lambda_i^1)\pi_i}{(\sum_i\lambda_i^2\pi_i)^2} \\ \frac{(\lambda_1^1\lambda_c^2-\lambda_1^2\lambda_c^1)(\sum_i\lambda_i^2\pi_i)-2\lambda_c^2(\sum_i(\lambda_1^1\lambda_i^2-\lambda_1^2\lambda_i^1)\pi_i)}{w_1^2(\sum_i\lambda_i^2\pi_i)^3} & w_c^1 & w_c^2 & \frac{\sum_i(\lambda_c^1\lambda_i^2-\lambda_c^2\lambda_i^1)\pi_i}{(\sum_i\lambda_i^2\pi_i)^2} \\ \frac{(\lambda_1^1\lambda_d^2-\lambda_1^2\lambda_d^1)(\sum_i\lambda_i^2\pi_i)-2\lambda_d^2(\sum_i(\lambda_1^1\lambda_i^2-\lambda_1^2\lambda_i^1)\pi_i)}{w_1^2(\sum_i\lambda_i^2\pi_i)^3} & w_d^1 & w_d^2 & \frac{\sum_i(\lambda_d^1\lambda_i^2-\lambda_d^2\lambda_i^1)\pi_i}{(\sum_i\lambda_i^2\pi_i)^2} \end{vmatrix} \tag{4.15}$$

The condition $\bar{D}_{a,b,c,d} = 0$ translates into a ninth degree polynomial in π being identically zero; all coefficients must therefore be zero, which requires a series of equalities in the parameters λ and w. But the set of parameters for which these equalities hold is of measure zero. Therefore identifiability obtains for 'almost all' values of the true parameters.

4.4 Application: Identifiability in the Collective Model ($H = 2$)

We may now specialize our result to specific economic contexts.

4.4.1 Identifiability With Purely Public Consumptions

We first consider the benchmark case where all commodities are publicly consumed; then $I = 0$ and $J = N$, and the problem can be expressed as:

$$P(X) = \sum_{h=1,2} \bar{\mu}^h(X) D_X U^h(X)$$

In that case, the exclusion assumption has a natural translation, namely that commodity 1 (resp. 2) does not enter the utility of member 1 (resp. 2). We conclude from Proposition 4.2 that U^1 and U^2 are ordinally identifiable. Moreover, for any cardinalization of these utilities, the coefficients μ^h are exactly identifiable. Since they are proportional to the Pareto weights and that the latter add up to one, we conclude that the Pareto weights are identifiable as well. In summary:

Corollary 4.3. In the collective model with two agents and public consumption only, if member 1 does not consume at least one item, then generically the utility of member 1 is exactly (ordinally) identifiable from household demand. If each member is the exclusive consumer of at least one item, then generically individual preferences are exactly (ordinally) identifiable from household demand; and for any cardinalization of individual utilities, the Pareto weights are exactly identifiable.

We may briefly discuss the conditions needed for identifiability. One is that $(\partial W^2(\pi)/\partial \pi_1) \neq 0$, i.e., in this case $(\partial U^2(\pi)/\partial X^1) \neq 0$. Clearly, if commodity one is valued neither by member 1 nor by member 2, household demand for this good is zero and cannot be used for identification.

More demanding is the requirement that $(\partial \theta/\partial X^1) \neq 0$. In our context, θ is the ratio of individual Pareto weights, expressed as a function of X; with the same notations as previously, we have that:

$$\theta(X) = \frac{\bar{\mu}^1(X)}{\bar{\mu}^2(X)} = \frac{\tilde{\mu}^1(P(X))}{\tilde{\mu}^2(P(X))}$$

where $\tilde{\mu}^h$ denotes the Pareto weight of h, expressed as a function of P. If we normalize $\tilde{\mu}^2(P)$ to be always equal to 1, finally $\theta(X) = \tilde{\mu}^1(P(X))$.

The partial $\partial\theta/\partial X^1$ is obviously zero if the first Pareto weight $\tilde{\mu}^1$ is constant. This is the case, discussed above, in which the household behaves as a single decision maker and maximizes the unitary utility $\mu U^1 + U^2$. If $\tilde{\mu}^1$ is not constant, however, then $\partial\theta/\partial X^1 = 0$ leads to the equation:

$$\sum_{k=1}^{N} \frac{\partial \tilde{\mu}}{\partial P_k}[P(X)]\frac{\partial P_k}{\partial X^1}(X) = 0$$

or equivalently:

$$\sum_{k=1}^{K} \frac{\partial \tilde{\mu}}{\partial P_k}(P)\varphi_k(P) = 0 \tag{4.16}$$

where the $\varphi_k, 1 \leq k \leq N$ are defined, using the implicit function theorem, by

$$\varphi_k(P(X)) = \frac{\partial P_k}{\partial X^1}(X)$$

Generically[3] in (μ, U^1, U^2), Equation (4.16) defines a submanifold Σ of codimension 1 (and hence a set of measure 0) in $\mathbb{R}^K$. In other words, for 'almost all' μ, U^1 and U^2 (in particular, if μ is not constant), there is a set Σ of measure 0 such that, whenever $P \notin \Sigma$, Pareto weights and preferences can be uniquely recovered from observing the collective demand function $X(P)$ near $\bar{P}$.

4.4.2 Application: Collective Models of Labor Supply with Public Consumptions

An immediate application is to the collective model of household labor supply, initially introduced by Chiappori (1988a,b, 1992). The idea is to consider the household as a two-person group making Pareto efficient decisions on consumption and labor supply; let L^h denote the leisure of member h, and w_h the corresponding wage. Various versions of the model can be considered. In each of them Corollary 4.3 applies, leading to full identifiability of the model.

(1) **Leisure as an exclusive good**

In the first model, each member's leisure is exclusively consumed by that member and there is no household production. Labor and non-labor incomes are used to

[3] Here, genericity is taken in the sense of Thom; it means that the set $\mathcal{N}$ of (μ, U^1, U^2) where the property does not hold is small in an appropriate sense. To be precise, it is, in an appropriate function space, a countable union of closed sets with empty interiors. As a consequence, it has itself an empty interior, so that if $(\bar{\mu}, \bar{U}^1, \bar{U}^2)$ happens to belong to $\mathcal{N}$, there are neighbours (μ, U^1, U^2), which are as close as one wishes to $(\bar{\mu}, \bar{U}^1, \bar{U}^2)$ and which do not belong to $\mathcal{N}$.

purchase commodities $X^1,\dots,X^K$ that are publicly consumed within the household; utilities are thus of the form $U^s(L^s,X^1,\dots,X^K)$.

(2) **Leisures are public, one exclusive good per member**

In the second model, leisure of one member is also consumed by the other member; again, there is no household production. The identifying assumption is that there exists two commodities (say, 1 and 2) such that commodity i does not enter the utility of member i.[4] One can think, for instance, of clothing as the exclusive commodity (as in Browning et al. 1994), but many other examples can be considered. Utilities are then of the form $U^h(L^1,L^2,X^h,X^3,\dots,X^K)$. Again, Proposition 4.3 applies: from the observation of the two labor supplies and the K consumptions as functions of prices, wages and non labor income, it is possible to uniquely recover preferences and Pareto weights. This is a strong result indeed, since it states that one can, from the sole observation of household labor supply and consumption, identify the partials $\partial U^i/\partial L^j$, $i \neq j$, that is, deduce to what extent individual leisures are publicly consumed.

(3) **Leisure as exclusive goods with household production**

As a third example, assume that individual time can be devoted to three different uses: leisure, market work and household production. The domestic good Y is produced from domestic labor under some constant return to scale technology, say $Y = f(t^1,t^2)$,[5] and publicly consumed within the household. Preferences are of the form $U^h(L^h,Y,X^1,\dots,X^K)$ and one can define

$$\tilde{U}^h(L^h,t^1,t^2,X^1,\dots,X^K) = U^h(L^h,f(t^1,t^2),X^1,\dots,X^K) \tag{4.17}$$

Here, Y is not observable in general, but t^1 and t^2 are observed, which typically requires data over time use

[4] This framework is close to (but less general than) that of Fong and Zhang (2000).

[5] Other inputs can be introduced at no cost, provided they are observable.

(obviously, there is little chance to identify household production if neither the output nor the input are observable). From Proposition 4.3, the $\tilde{U}^h$ are identified. Then the production function can be recovered up to a scaling factor, using the assumption of constant return to scale, from the relation:

$$\frac{\partial \tilde{U}^1/\partial t^1}{\partial \tilde{U}^1/\partial t^2} = \frac{\partial \tilde{U}^2/\partial t^1}{\partial \tilde{U}^2/\partial t^2} = \frac{\partial f/\partial t^1}{\partial f/\partial t^2}$$

which in addition generates an overidentifying restriction. Finally, (4.17) allows to recover the U^h; again, the separability property in (4.17) generates additional, testable restrictions.

(4) **Leisures are public, one exclusive good per member and household production**

Finally, one can combine models 2 and 3 by assuming that leisure is a public good, but the demand for two other exclusive goods can be observed. Again, identifiability generically obtains in this context.

4.4.3 Identifiability in the General Case

We may now address the general case with private and public consumptions. For convenience, we abandon for a while the normalization $y = 1$; hence all functions are functions of (p, X, y). In particular, the group's total expenditures on public goods are now $A(p, X, y) = P(p, X, y)^{\mathrm{T}} \cdot X$.

In the presence of private consumption, the problem is more complex, because the exclusion assumption introduced in Proposition 4.2 does not have a direct economic translation. Indeed, remember that:

$$W^h(p, X, y) = V^h(p, X, \rho^h(p, X, y))$$

hence:

$$\frac{\partial W^1}{\partial p_1} = \frac{\partial V^1}{\partial p_1} + \frac{\partial V^1}{\partial \rho^1}\frac{\partial \rho^1}{\partial p_1}$$

We see, in particular, that even when consumer 1 does not consume commodity 1, so that $(\partial V^1/\partial p_1) = (\partial U^1/\partial X^1) = 0$, we still have that $(\partial W^1/\partial p_1) = (\partial V^1/\partial \rho)(\partial \rho^1/\partial p_1) \neq 0$ in general. Intuitively, even when a commodity is not consumed by an agent, the corresponding expenditures may still impact the agent's share of resources, therefore the agent's welfare, through an income effect.

However, Corollary 4.2 is now the relevant tool. Take a point $(\bar{p}, \bar{X}, \bar{y})$ and assume that:

$$\frac{\partial \rho^1}{\partial y}(\bar{p}, \bar{X}, \bar{y}) \neq 0. \tag{4.18}$$

From now on, all results are understood to be local, that is, to hold in some neighborhood of $(\bar{p}, \bar{X}, \bar{y})$.

Assume now that commodity 1 is not consumed by member 1, and commodity 2 is not consumed by member 2:

$$\frac{\partial V^i}{\partial p_i} = \frac{\partial U^i}{\partial X^i} = 0, \quad i = 1, 2$$

It follows, first, that for any solution W:

$$\frac{\partial W^1(p, X, y)/\partial p_1}{\partial W^1(p, X, y)/\partial y} = \frac{\partial \rho^1(p, X, y)/\partial p_1}{\partial \rho^1(p, X, y)/\partial y}$$

Let $(U^1, U^2, \rho^1, \rho^2 = y - A - \rho^1)$ and $(\bar{U}^1, \bar{U}^2, \bar{\rho}^1, \bar{\rho}^2 = y - A - \bar{\rho}^1)$ be the utilities and conditional sharing rules corresponding to two different solutions of Equation (3.24). We have:

$$\frac{\partial W^1/\partial p_1}{\partial W^1/\partial y} = \frac{\partial \rho^1/\partial p_1}{\partial \rho^1/\partial y} \quad \text{and} \quad \frac{\partial \bar{W}^1/\partial p_1}{\partial \bar{W}^1/\partial y} = \frac{\partial \bar{\rho}^1/\partial p_1}{\partial \bar{\rho}^1/\partial y} \tag{4.19}$$

Consider the household demand x_1 for commodity 2. We have:

$$\begin{aligned} x_2(p, X, y) &= \xi_2^1(p_2, \ldots, p_n, X, \rho^1(p, X, y)) \\ &= \bar{\xi}_2^1(p_2, \ldots, p_n, X, \bar{\rho}^1(p, X, y)) \end{aligned}$$

where ξ_i^1 (resp. $\bar{\xi}_i^1$) is the conditional Marshallian demand corresponding to U^1 (resp. $\bar{U}^1$). Therefore:

$$\frac{\partial \rho^1/\partial p_1}{\partial \rho^1/\partial y} = \frac{\partial x_2/\partial p_1}{\partial x_i/\partial y} = \frac{\partial \bar{\rho}^1/\partial p_1}{\partial \bar{\rho}^1/\partial y}. \tag{4.20}$$

Comparing (4.19) with (4.20), we get:

$$\frac{\partial \bar{W}/\partial p_1}{\partial \bar{W}^1/\partial y} = \frac{\partial \rho^1/\partial p_1}{\partial \rho^1/\partial y}$$

which is condition (4.12). Applying Corollary 4.2, we get:

Corollary 4.4. In the general, collective model with two agents, under assumption (4.18), if each member does not consume at least one good, then generically the indirect collective utility of each member is exactly (ordinally) identifiable from household demand. For any cardinalization of indirect collective utilities, the Pareto weights are exactly identifiable.

Note, however, that the conditions (4.5) have to be satisfied. Although they hold true in a 'generic' sense, checking that they are fulfilled in a specific context may be tedious. In such cases, using distribution factors may facilitate identifiability (see below).

Links with the existing literature. The statements derived above provide a general framework, of which several particular cases can be found in the literature. For instance, Chiappori (1992) analyzes a collective model of labor supply in three goods framework (two labor supplies and an Hicksian composite good). In this model, all commodities are privately consumed, and each member's labor supply is exclusive. More recently, Blundell et al., consider a similar model, with the difference that the non exclusive good is public (and can be interpreted as children expenditures or welfare). They prove that their model is generically identifiable.[6]

4.4.4 Identifiability Using Distribution Factors

The results derived so far do not use distribution factors. We now show how such factors can help the identification process by alleviating the necessary conditions required. Let z denote a distribution factor which is behavior relevant, in the sense that $\partial\theta/\partial z \neq 0$ where $\theta = \mu^1/\mu^2$ as usual. Also, we maintain the regularity assumption (4.18). From:

$$W^1(p, X, y, z) = V^1(p, X, \rho^1(p, X, y, z))$$

[6] BCM provide a detailed analysis of the comparative statics of such a model and of its welfare implications. They show, in particular, that increasing the Pareto weight of a particular member increases the household demand for a public item if and only if the person's marginal willingness to pay for the public item is more income sensitive than that of her spouse.

we get that:

$$\frac{\partial W^1/\partial z}{\partial W^1/\partial y} = \frac{\partial \rho^1/\partial z}{\partial \rho^1/\partial y} \tag{4.21}$$

and Corollary 4.2 applies if we can show that the right-hand side does not depend on the particular solution considered. This can be done, as before, when each member does not consume (at least) one commodity. But this requirement can be relaxed. We only need either one excluded item (instead of two) or an *assignable* commodity. An item is assignable when it is consumed by both members, and the consumption of each member is independently observed.

Assume that item 1 is either assignable or exclusively consumed by member 1, so that $x_1^1(p, X, y, z)$ is observed. Now, for any two solutions, we have that

$$x_1^1(p, X, y, z) = \xi_1^1(p, X, \rho^1(p, X, y, z)) = \bar{\xi}_1^1(p, X, \bar{\rho}^1(p, X, y, z))$$

where ξ_1^1 and $\bar{\xi}_1^1$ denote the conditional demand of member 1 in each solution. Therefore:

$$\frac{\partial \rho^1/\partial z}{\partial \rho^1/\partial y} = \frac{\partial x_1^1/\partial z}{\partial x_1^1/\partial y} = \frac{\partial \bar{\rho}^1/\partial z}{\partial \bar{\rho}^1/\partial y}$$

and the right-hand side of Equation (4.21) does not depend on the particular solution considered, so that identifiability obtains by Corollary 4.2.

The genericity condition (4.5) may also be easier to check in that case. Consider, in particular, the case of private goods only. Then

$$W^2(p, y, z) = V^2(p, \rho^2(p, y, z)) = V^2(p, y - \rho^1(p, y, z))$$

hence:

$$\frac{\partial W^2/\partial z}{\partial W^2/\partial y} = \frac{\partial \rho^2/\partial z}{\partial \rho^2/\partial y} = -\frac{\partial \rho^1/\partial z}{1 - \partial \rho^1/\partial y}$$

which cannot equal $(\partial \rho^1/\partial z/\partial \rho^1/\partial y)$ unless $\partial \rho^1/\partial z = 0$, i.e., unless the distribution factor is behavior irrelevant.

4.5 The General Case ($H \geq 2$)

Finally, how do these results generalize to groups of arbitrary sizes? We only indicate here the main results. First, Lemma 7.17 extends as follows. Consider the equation

$$\xi(\pi) = \sum_{h=1}^{H} \lambda^h(\pi) D_\pi W^h$$

where $\pi \in \mathbb{R}^N$ and ξ maps $\mathbb{R}^N$ into itself. Let $(\bar{W}^1, \ldots, \bar{W}^H, \bar{\lambda}^1, \ldots, \bar{\lambda}^H)$ be a particular solution. Under a regularity condition, for any other solution $(W^1, \ldots, W^H, \lambda^1, \ldots, \lambda^H)$, there exists H continuous functions $F^1, \ldots, F^H$ such that:

$$W^1(\pi) = F^1\left[\bar{W}^1, \ldots, \bar{W}^H, \frac{\bar{\lambda}^1}{\bar{\lambda}^H}, \ldots, \frac{\bar{\lambda}^{H-1}}{\bar{\lambda}^H}\right]$$

$$\vdots$$

$$W^H(\pi) = F^H\left[\bar{W}^1, \ldots, \bar{W}^H, \frac{\bar{\lambda}^1}{\bar{\lambda}^H}, \ldots, \frac{\bar{\lambda}^{H-1}}{\bar{\lambda}^H}\right]$$

where the F^h satisfy moreover a set of partial differential equations. Secondly, identifiability under exclusion still holds in the following sense. Assume that there exists some variables, say $\pi_1, \pi_2, \ldots, \pi_S$, such that $(\partial W^h / \partial \pi_h) = 0$ for all $h \geq 1$. Then generically $W^1, \ldots, W^S$ are identifiable in the ordinal sense. The generalized separability property extends in a similar manner.

Regarding economic implications, we conclude that while the general model (without exclusion) is clearly not identifiable, one consumption exclusion per agent is sufficient to obtain generic identifiability in the general case, with the same caveats as above. The techniques are similar to (although more tedious than) those used above.

Perhaps more important is the conclusion in the presence of *one* distribution factor (at least). Indeed, the argument previously described for two agents directly extends to $S \geq 2$. For any two solutions W^s and $\bar{W}^s$, we have that

$$\frac{\partial W^s / \partial z}{\partial W^s / \partial y} = \frac{\partial x_s^1 / \partial z}{\partial x_s^1 / \partial y} = \frac{\partial \bar{W}^s / \partial z}{\partial \bar{W}^s / \partial y}$$

Provided that the genericity conditions are satisfied (in particular, the $(\partial \rho^s / \partial z)/(\partial \rho^s / \partial y)$ must be pairwise different), we then conclude that the W^s are (ordinally) exactly identified, without restriction on the number of distribution factors.

4.6 Empirical Implementation

The above results deal with identifiability from what could be called 'ideal data' — i.e., a continuous (actually differentiable) demand function. What about actual identification of an identifiable model? Specifically, what type of stochastic structure should be used, and to what (finite) data can it be applied?

Data set are readily available (and have been used) for models of household labor supply. An abundant literature already exists on that topic; the reader is referred to Fortin and Lacroix (1997); Chiappori et al. (2002); Donni (2003); Laisney (2004); Vermeulen (2005) among many others.

The case of consumption goods is somewhat different. A standard problem of demand analysis is that while income effects are usually easy to estimate, the measurement of price effects require price variations, which may be hard to obtain. Two strategies have been used in the literature. One relies on variations through time and regions (see for instance Browning and Chiappori (1998) and Browning et al. (2005). Alternatively, one may use natural experiments to generate exogenous price variations. For instance, Kapan (2009) uses Turkish data collected in a period of high inflation; similar households then face widely different relative prices depending on the month during which they are surveyed. Both works reject the unitary model when applied to couples, but not for singles; moreover, none rejects the collective model for couples.

Regarding the stochastic structure, on the other hand, existing works use mostly the standard approach of consumer theory, in which stochastic error terms (reflecting measurement errors, but also unobserved heterogeneity, etc.) enter demand equations additively. Identification is in general easy to achieve in this context. Some models, however consider more sophisticated stochastic structure, and discuss the related identification issues; see Blundell et al. (2000) in the case of labor supply.

All in all, it is fair to conclude that much still has to be done in terms of empirical applications of the collective model. The main goal of the present paper is to provide a theoretical background for such works. One thing seems however clear: whenever issues related to intra-household allocation of commodities, welfare or decision power are at stake, non-unitary models are needed. The collective approach provides a consistent and promising theoretical framework for that purpose.

5

Aggregation in Market Economies

One very particular case of the collective model developed above has attracted considerable attention in the literature. It relies on the following assumptions:

(1) All commodities are privately consumed, and preferences are egoistic. In particular, interactions between group members (if any) are restricted to commodity trading.
(2) Individuals each maximize their own utility under a budget constraint of the form:

$$\max_{x_h} U^h(x_h) \quad \text{subject to } p^{\mathrm{T}} x_h = y^h(p) \tag{5.1}$$

where $y(p) = (y^1(p), \ldots, y^H(p))$ is some *exogenously given* income allocation

Clearly, the resulting allocation is Pareto efficient (this is a straightforward consequence of standard welfare theorems). Conversely, we know that in a private good context, for any efficient allocation one can find a sharing rule $y(p) = (y^1(p), \ldots, y^H(p))$, with $\sum_h y^h(p) = H$, such that each individual consumption solves (5.1).

The crucial aspect of the problem we consider in this section is that, *in addition*, we impose a specific form for the sharing rule. Specifically, two forms have been considered in the literature:

(a) Constant nominal income: $y^h(p) = y^h \in \mathbb{R}$ for all p, h
(b) Proportional income: $y^h(p) = p^{\mathrm{T}} \cdot \omega^h$, where $\omega^h \in \mathbb{R}^N$.

Case (a) corresponds to the *market demand* problem. Its interpretation is straightforward; it amounts to considering an economy in which each agent is initially endowed with some fixed monetary income y^h. The interpretation of case (b) is similar, except that agents are endowed with a commodity bundle ω^h, the value of which depends on the prevailing vector; what is considered is the agent's *excess demand*, defined as the difference between the agent's desired consumption bundle and her initial endowment.

In both cases, aggregate demand depends on prices and initial endowments. The main question, however, is the characterization of aggregate demand *as a function of prices*. It can therefore be stated as follows: *consider a given function $x(p)$. When is it possible to find H smooth, increasing, strongly concave utility functions U^h such that*

- *(market demand)*

$$x(p) = \sum_h x_h(p)$$

where $x_h(p)$ solves

$$\max_{x_h} U^h(x_h) \quad \text{subject to } p^{\mathrm{T}} x_h \leq y^h \tag{5.2}$$

- *(excess demand)*

$$x(p) = \sum_h (x_h(p) - \omega^h)$$

where $x_h(p)$ solves

$$\max_{x_h} U^h(x_h) \quad \text{subject to } p^{\mathrm{T}} x_h \leq p^{\mathrm{T}} \omega^h \tag{5.3}$$

There exists obvious properties that the aggregate market or excess demand will satisfy. One is continuity (or differentiability in our context). Another is adding-up (sometimes called Walras Law); namely, it must be the case that $p^{\mathrm{T}}x(p) = \sum_h y^h = H$ for market demand, and $p^{\mathrm{T}}x(p) = \sum_h p^{\mathrm{T}}(x_h(p) - \omega^h) = 0$ for excess demand. Finally, excess demand functions are zero-homogeneous in prices. The question is whether these properties are sufficient, or whether the underlying structure generates stronger properties at the aggregate level.

In practice, a large fraction of the literature is devoted to the case of 'many agents' — i.e., when the number of agents is larger than the number of commodities, while a few works consider the case of a 'small' number of agents. We shall study both cases in what follows.

5.1 Aggregate Excess Demand With Many Agents

We start with the simplest case, namely the structure of a group's aggregate excess demand when the number of agents is 'large'. Note, first, that for any given set of direct utilities $\{U^1,\ldots,U^H\}$ and initial endowments $\{\omega^1,\ldots,\omega^H\}$, one can define the utilities $\{\tilde{U}^1,\ldots,\tilde{U}^H\}$ by $\tilde{U}^h(z) = U^h(z+\omega^h)$, $h = 1,\ldots,H$; intuitively, $\tilde{U}^h$ is the utility generated by a given, *excess* demand vector. With this notation, Program (5.3) can be rewritten as:

$$\max_z \tilde{U}^h(z) \text{ subject to } p^{\mathrm{T}}z \leq 0 \tag{5.4}$$

and we define the indirect utility V^h as the value of program (5.4):

$$V^h(p) = \{\max_z \tilde{U}^h(z) \mid z \in \mathbb{R}^N,\, p^{\mathrm{T}}z \leq 0\} \tag{5.5}$$

An important property of Program 5.4, that will play a key role below, is that the indirect utility function V^h is positively homogeneous of degree zero: $V^h(\lambda p) = V^h(p)$ for all $\lambda > 0$. This is in sharp contrast with the market demand case, in which no such property holds. As a consequence, the correspondence between $\tilde{U}^h$ and V^h is not one-to-one: for any choice of $\lambda > 0$, the function $\tilde{U}^h(\lambda z)$ yields the same indirect utility as $\tilde{U}^h(z)$. So formula (5.5) cannot be inverted: we need additional information to determine $\tilde{U}^h$ from V^h. The following lemma, from Chiappori and Ekeland (1999b), shows that we all need is a positive function $\lambda(p)$, which can be chosen arbitrarily:

Lemma 5.1. Let $V(p)$ be a C^3 function defined on some neighborhood $\mathcal{O}$ of $\bar{p}$, with $D_pV(\bar{p}) \neq 0$. Assume that it is quasi-convex, positively homogeneous of degree zero, that $D^2_{pp}V(p)$ has rank $(N-1)$ and that the restriction of $D^2_{pp}V(p)$ to $\mathrm{Span}\{p, D_pV(p)\}^{\perp}$ is positive definite. Take any C^2 function $\lambda(p) > 0$, homogeneous of degree (-1) on $\mathcal{O}$, and set:

$$z(p) = -\frac{1}{\lambda(p)} D_pV(p) \tag{5.6}$$

so that $p^{\mathrm{T}} z(p) = 0$. Then there is a strictly quasi-concave function $U(z)$, defined and C^2 in a neighborhood $\mathcal{N}$ of $z(\bar{p})$, such that V is the indirect utility associated with U, namely:

(1) For every $z \in \mathcal{N}$, the restriction of $D^2_{zz}U(z)$ to $[D_zU(z)]^{\perp}$ is negative definite
(2) For every $p \in \mathcal{O}$, we have:

$$D_zU(z(p)) = \lambda(p)p, \tag{5.7}$$

$$V(p) = U(z(p)) = \max_z\{U(z) \mid p^{\mathrm{T}} z \leq 0\} \tag{5.8}$$

The conditions on V are also necessary: if U is strictly quasi-concave[1], then it follows from formula (5.5) that V is quasi-convex, positively homogeneous of degree zero, that the $D^2_{pp}V(p)$ has rank at most $(N-1)$ and that the restriction of $D^2_{pp}V(p)$ to $\mathrm{Span}\{p, D_pV(p)\}^{\perp}$ is positive definite.

The main result in this literature, initially proved by Debreu and by Mantel, both in 1974, states that the trivial conditions (continuity, homogeneity, adding-up) fully characterize the excess demand function of a large economy; that is, *any* smooth function satisfying homogeneity

[1] More precisely, we require that $DU^h(\zeta)$ be non-zero and that the restriction of the second derivative $D^2U^h(\zeta)$ to $[DU^h(\zeta)]^{\perp}$ is negative definite for every ζ.

and adding up can be decomposed as the excess demand of a well-constructed economy. We give here a slightly stronger statement due to Chiappori and Ekeland (1999a,b). Note that the decomposition $x(p) = \sum_h (x_h(p) - \omega^h)$ will be shown to hold on a given set K of $p \in \mathbb{R}^{\mathbf{N}}_{++}$, and not on an unspecified neighborhood of some given point $\bar{p}$. On the other hand, there are restrictions on the set K: it is not allowed to touch the boundary of $\mathbb{R}^{\mathbf{N}}_{++}$, or even to approach it asymptotically; one could remove these restrictions, but then one would have to specify the behavior of $x(p)$ when one of the relative prices goes to zero.

Let us start with some notations. Because of homogeneity, we can normalize prices; following the literature, we therefore impose that $p^{\mathrm{T}}p = 1$, so that prices belong to $\mathbb{R}^N_{++} \cap S^{N-1}$, where S^{N-1} is the sphere in $\mathbb{R}^N$. Since $p^{\mathrm{T}}x(p) = 0$, we can think of $x(p)$ as a tangent vector to $S^{\mathbf{N}-1}$ at p; the space of all such vectors (the tangent space $T_pS^{\mathbf{N}-1}$ to $S^{\mathbf{N}-1}$ at p) has dimension $(\mathbf{N} - 1)$.

In what follows, K denotes some compact subset included in the interior of $\mathbb{R}^{\mathbf{N}}_{++} \cap S^{\mathbf{N}-1}$, and $H \geq N$ is given.

Definition 5.1. We shall say that a family $V^h(p), 1 \leq h \leq H$, of functions defined on $\mathbb{R}^{\mathbf{N}}_{++}$ is *normal* if:

(1) Each of the $V^h(p)$ is C^3, quasi-convex and positively homogenous of degree zero.
(2) For every $p \in K$ and every h, $D^2_{pp}V^h(p)$ has maximal rank $(N - 1)$, and the restriction of $D^2_{pp}V^h(p)$ to $[\mathrm{Span}\{p, D_pV^h(p)\}]^{\perp}$ is positive definite.
(3) If $D_pV^h(p_1)$ and $D_pV^h(p_2)$ are collinear, with p_1 and p_2 in K, so are p_1 and p_2.
(4) At every $p \in K$, the set of linear combination of the $DV^h(p)$ with non negative coefficients spans $T_pS^{\mathbf{N}-1}$.

Theorem 5.2. Suppose that the family $V^h(p), 1 \leq h \leq H$ is normal. Then, for any C^2 map $x(p)$ defined on K , homogeneous of degree zero and satisfying the Walras law $p^{\mathrm{T}}x(p) = 0$, one can find excess demand functions $z_h(p), 1 \leq h \leq H$, such that the decomposition

$x(p) = \sum_h z_h(p)$ holds on K and the indirect utility associated to z_h is V^h.

This version of the result is slightly stronger than the initial one because the indirect utilities can be defined independently of the excess demand at stake; i.e., the *same* $V^1(p),\ldots,V^H(p)$ can be used in the decomposition of any given function. This property may sound surprising. It reflects the fact that, in sharp contrast with market demands, there exists a continuum of individual excess demands that correspond to the same indirect utility (of course, they involve different initial endowments in general).

The initial proof, as provided by Debreu (1974) and Mantel (1974), was quite complex. In fact, the result is surprisingly easy to show. The basic ingredient is the following lemma.

Lemma 5.3. Assume that $z(p)$ is an individual excess demand function, that is, that there exists a smooth, increasing, strongly concave utility function U and a non negative vector ω such that $z(p) = x(p) - \omega$, where $x(p)$ solves:

$$\max_x U(x) \text{ subject to } p^{\mathrm{T}} x = p^{\mathrm{T}} \omega$$

Pick any non-negative scalar function $\lambda(p)$; then $\lambda(p)z(p)$ also is an individual excess demand function.

Proof. A detailed proof, based on Lemma 5.1, can be found in Chiappori and Ekeland (2004). Incidentally, a different proof, based on a revealed preferences argument, has been known since Debreu (1974). The strong axiom of revealed preferences, applied to individual excess demand functions, states that whenever one can find k price vectors $p^1,\ldots,p^k$ such that $(p^1)^{\mathrm{T}} z(p^2) \leq 0,\ldots,(p^{k-1})^{\mathrm{T}} z(p^k) \leq 0$ then necessarily $(p^k)^{\mathrm{T}} z(p^1) > 0$. Clearly, if this property holds for $z(p)$ it also holds for $\lambda(p)z(p)$. □

Now, pick $H \geq N$ individual excess demand $z_1(p),\ldots,z_H(p)$ such that, at every $p \in K$, the set of linear combination of the $z_h(p)$ with non-negative coefficients spans $T_p S^{\mathbf{N}-1}$. Then any map $z(p)$ defined on K , homogeneous of degree zero and satisfying the Walras law $p^{\mathrm{T}}z(p) = 0$ can be decomposed as

$$z(p) = \sum_{h=1}^{H} \lambda_h(p) z_h(p)$$

with $\lambda_h(p) \geq 0$ for all h. By Lemma 5.3, $\lambda_h(p)z_h(p)$ is an individual excess demand function.

It remains to find H individual excess demands such that, at every $p \in K$, the set of linear combination of the $z_h(p)$ with non-negative coefficients spans $T_p S^{\mathbf{N}-1}$. To do this, note first that the two following conditions are equivalent:

(1) The convex cone generated by n vectors $(e_1,\ldots,e_N)$ in $\mathbb{R}^{\mathbf{N}-1}$ is $\mathbb{R}^{\mathbf{N}-1}$.
(2) The convex hull of $(e_1,\ldots,e_N)$ contains 0.

Now, consider for instance the functions:

$$V_h(p) = \left(\frac{p_h}{\sum_k p_k} - 1\right)^2 + \sum_{j \neq h} \left(\frac{p_j}{\sum_k p_k}\right)^2$$

and define $z_h(p) = D_p V_h(p)$. One can readily show that z_h is an individual excess demand, and that the convex hull of the $z_h(p)$ in $[p]^{\perp}$ contains 0 in its interior. So the convex cone spanned by the $z_h(p)$ is $T_p S^{\mathbf{N}-1}$. The reader is referred to Chiappori and Ekeland for a detailed presentation.

Finally, note that the restriction $H \geq N$ is needed because we want a global result. If we are content to have a decomposition valid only in a neighborhood of $\bar{p}$, then $H \geq N - 1$ is sufficient: we can always choose $V^h, 1 \leq h \leq N-1$ so that $z(\bar{p})$ is a linear combination of the $D_p V^h(\bar{p})$ with positive coefficients, and these coefficients will remain positive in some neighborhood of $\bar{p}$.

5.2 Aggregate Market Demand With Many Agents

The second problem — a group's aggregate *market* demand when the number of agents is 'large' — is surprisingly difficult; much more, as it turns out, than the excess demand case. No simple proof (similar to the one described above) exists; the full strength of Cartan-Kähler theorem is required (see Theorem 7.27)

5.2.1 The Main Result

In the market demand case, individual h is endowed with some given nominal income y^h. In what follows, we assume that $y^h = 1$; this simplifies the notations without reducing the generality of the proof, which can readily be extended to any vector $y = (y^1, \dots, y^H)$. In what follows, we assume that $H \geq N$.

Formally, consider some mapping $x(p)$ from $\mathbb{R}^N$ to itself. We want to decompose it into the sum of H individual market demand functions:

$$x(p) = x_1(p) + \cdots + x_H(p) \tag{5.9}$$

such that for all h, $x_h(p)$ solves

$$\max U^h(x) \, p^{\mathrm{T}} x = 1 \tag{5.10}$$

where U^h is 'smooth' (in a sense that will be discussed below), strongly convex and strictly increasing.

Note that (5.10) is identical to (5.4) — and therefore the market demand problem similar to the excess demand one — except for one detail — namely, the individual budget constraint is $p^{\mathrm{T}} x = 1$ instead of $p^{\mathrm{T}} z = 0$. As it turns out, this apparently minor variation results in a considerably more difficult problem. As mentioned above, an obvious but crucial property of a constraint like $p^{\mathrm{T}} z = 0$ is that if it is satisfied by some function z, then it is also satisfied by $\lambda \cdot z$ for any scalar function λ. No such property exists in the present context.

As before, the indirect utility of agent h is defined as the value of Program (5.10):

$$V^h(p) = \max_x \{U^h(x) \mid p^{\mathrm{T}} x = 1\} \tag{5.11}$$

By the envelope theorem,

$$D_p V^h = -\lambda^h x_h(p) \tag{5.12}$$

where λ^h is the Lagrange multiplier of the budget constraint in (5.10) and $x_h(p)$ is the solution of Program (5.11).

The main result is then the (Chiappori and Ekeland, 1999a):

Theorem 5.4. Suppose $H \geq N$. Consider some open set $\mathcal{U}$ in $\mathbb{R}^N \backslash \{0\}$ and some analytic map $x: U \to \mathbb{R}^N$ such that $p^{\mathrm{T}} x(p) = H$. For all $\bar{p} \in U$, all $(\bar{x}_1, \ldots, \bar{x}_H) \in \mathbb{R}^{nH}$ and all $(\bar{\lambda}^1, \ldots, \bar{\lambda}^H) \in \mathbb{R}^H$ that satisfy:

$$\bar{x}_1 + \cdots + \bar{x}_H = x(\bar{p}) \quad \forall i, \quad \bar{\lambda}^h > 0$$

there exist H functions $U^1, \ldots, U^H$, where each U^h is defined in some convex neighborhood $\mathcal{U}_h$ of $\bar{x}_h$ and is analytic and strictly concave, H mappings $(x_1, \ldots, x_H)$ and H functions $(\lambda^1, \ldots, \lambda^H)$, all defined in some neighborhood V of $\bar{p}$ and analytic in V, such that, for all $p \in V$:

$$\begin{aligned}
p^{\mathrm{T}} x_h(p) &= 1, \quad h = 1, \ldots, H \\
U^h(x_h(p)) &= \max\{U^h(x) \mid x \in \mathcal{U}^h, p^{\mathrm{T}} x \leq 1\}, \quad h = 1, \ldots, H \\
\frac{\partial U^h}{\partial x^j}(x_h(p)) &= \lambda^h(p) p_j, \quad h = 1, \ldots, H, \ j = 1, \ldots, N \\
\sum_{h=1}^{H} x_h(p) &= x(p) \\
x_h(\bar{p}) &= \bar{x}_h, \quad h = 1, \ldots, H \\
\lambda^h(\bar{p}) &= \bar{\lambda}^h, \quad h = 1, \ldots, H
\end{aligned}$$

Before proving this result, let us delve upon the analyticity requirement. The function $x(p)$ that has to be decomposed into an aggregate demand must be analytic, which means that (a) at every point its Taylor expansion must be summable, and (b) within the radius of convergence, the function must be equal to its Taylor expansion at that point (see Definition 7.7). This is a much stronger requirement than asking that $x(p)$ be C^∞. Polynomials in $(p_1, \ldots, p_N)$ are analytic on $\mathbb{R}^N$, functions of the form F/G, where $F(p)$ and $G(p)$ are polynomials on $\mathbb{R}^N \backslash \Omega$, where Ω is the set of zeros of G, the norm $\|p\|$ is analytic on $\mathbb{R}^N \backslash \{0\}$, and so are all the elementary functions. One can think of an analytic function as one for which there exists an explicit formula. However, mathematically speaking, most C^∞ functions are not analytic. The classical example of a C^∞, non-analytic function on $\mathbb{R}$ is the following:

$$f(t) = \begin{cases} \exp(-\frac{1}{t^2}), & \text{for } t > 0 \\ 0, & \text{for } t \leq 0 \end{cases}$$

Note that f is C^∞ in any neighborhood of the origin, and all its derivatives at 0 vanish. So the Taylor series at 0 sums to 0, which proves that f cannot be analytic, because it does not coincide with the sum of its Taylor expansion.

The reason for analyticity is mathematical: in essence, the strategy of the proof boils down to proving that certain system of partial differential equations has a solution (fulfilling additional convexity requirements), and the only general tool that can be applied to such systems is the so-called Cauchy–Kowalewska Theorem, which requires analyticity. In highly specific cases, such as the excess demand problem, the difficulty can be by-passed exploiting some specificities of the structure at stake. Here, however, no such shortcut seems to exist.

From the economic point of view, the difference between a C^∞ and analytic would seem to fine to make any practical difference. After all, any C^∞ function can be approximated by polynomials (which are analytic functions) uniformly on compact sets. So, if the aggregate demand function $x(p)$ is C^∞ and not analytic, one can approximate it by a sequence of analytic functions $x^n(p), n \in \mathbb{N}$, apply Theorem 5.4 to each of the x^n, decomposing it as $\sum_{h=1}^{H} x_h^n(p) = x^n(p)$, and let $n \longrightarrow \infty$: surely then, since $x^n(p)$ converges to $x(p)$, it must be the case that $x_h^n(p)$ converges to some $x_h(p)$ for every h? Unfortunately, that is wrong for many systems of partial differential equations: the $x_h(p)$ may just blow up without converging to anything. This phenomenon was discovered by the French mathematician Hadamard in the beginning of the twentieth century, and such problems are now referred to as "ill-posed in the sense of Hadamard". Whether the problem at hand falls into that category is something we have been unable to find out. So let us just warn the reader that we do not know whether the utilities $U_h(x)$ given by Theorem 5.4 depend continuously on the observation $x(p)$.

5.2.2 Proof of Theorem 5.4: The Strategy

We do not provide here a complete proof; the reader is referred to Chiappori and Ekeland (1999a). However, for the sake of completeness, we briefly described the main strategy of the proof. The argument is in three steps. It is clearly enough to prove the theorem for $H = N$, which we assume from now on.

5.2.2.1 Step 1: Reduce the problem to a system of PDEs

Substituting (5.12) into (5.9), we get:

$$x(p) = -\sum_{h=1}^{N} \frac{1}{\lambda^h(p)} D_p V^h(p) \tag{5.13}$$

In addition, we adjoin the condition $p^{\mathrm{T}} \bar{x}_h(p) = 1$, which yields:

$$p^{\mathrm{T}} DV^h(p) = -\lambda^h(p), \quad h = 1,..,N \tag{5.14}$$

We now restate the problem as follows: given an analytic map $x(p)$, satisfying $p^{\mathrm{T}} x(p) = H$, find convex functions $V^1,\ldots,V^N$ and positive functions $\lambda^1,\ldots,\lambda^N$ satisfying Equations (5.13) and (5.14).

We can eliminate the λ^h by computing them from Equation (5.14) and writing the result in Equation (5.13). We get a system of N equations for the N unknown functions V^h:

$$\sum_{h=1}^{N} \frac{DV^h(p)}{p^{\mathrm{T}} DV^h(p)} = -x(p) \tag{5.15}$$

5.2.2.2 Step 2: Reduce the problem to an exterior differential system

We first make the transformation $\mu^h := -1/\lambda^h$, so that the system becomes:

$$\begin{array}{c} \sum_{h=1}^{N} \mu^h(p) D_p V^h(p) = x(p) \\ p^{\mathrm{T}} DV^h(p) = -1/\mu^h(p), \quad h = 1,..,N \end{array} \tag{5.16}$$

Introduce the space:

$$E = \mathbb{R}^{N+N+N^2} = \{(p_n, \mu^h, \Delta_{h'}^{n'}) \mid 1 \le n, n' \le N, 1 \le h, h' \le N\}$$

In this space, consider the submanifold $\mathcal{M}$ defined by the equations:

$$\begin{aligned} \textstyle\sum_h \mu^h \Delta_h^n &= x^n(p), \quad \forall n, \\ \textstyle\sum_n p_n \Delta_h^n &= -1/\mu^h, \quad \forall h. \end{aligned} \tag{5.17}$$

The equations are independent, so that $\mathcal{M}$ is a submanifold of codimension $2N$, and hence dimension N^2. In $\mathcal{M}$ (and *not* in E) we consider the exterior differential system (EDS):

$$\begin{aligned} \textstyle\sum_n d\Delta_h^n \wedge dp_n &= 0, \quad \forall h, \\ dp_1 \wedge \cdots \wedge dp_N &= 0 \end{aligned} \tag{5.18}$$

This EDS is equivalent to the system (5.16). An integral manifold of Equation (5.18) is the graph of a map $(\Delta_h^n(p), \mu^h(p)), 1 \leq h \leq N$: by the Poincaré lemma (Proposition 7.8), the equation $\sum_n d\Delta_h^n \wedge dp_n = 0$ means that $\Delta_h^n(p) = \partial V^h / \partial p_k$ for some function V^h. We have now set the stage for the Cartan–Kähler theorem.

5.2.2.3 Step 3: Solve the *linearized* problem

We now consider a linearized version of the system at some given point $\bar{p}$. Set $\mu^h := 1/\lambda^h$. Then one must choose the values of μ^h and $\Delta^h = D_p V^h$ at $\bar{p}$, say, $\bar{\mu}^h$ and $\bar{\Delta}^h$, so that $\bar{\mu}^h < 0$, $\bar{\Delta}^h << 0$, $\bar{\Delta} = (\bar{\Delta}^1, \ldots, \bar{\Delta}^N)$ is invertible (note that if these properties hold at $\bar{p}$, they will hold by continuity in a neighborhood as well), and such that these values satisfy the relations:

$$\sum_h \bar{\mu}^h \bar{\Delta}^h = X(\bar{p})$$

and

$$\bar{p}^{\mathrm{T}} \bar{\Delta}^h = -1/\bar{\mu}^h \quad \forall h$$

Now, we linearize μ^h and Δ^h (as functions of p) around $\bar{p}$:

$$\frac{\partial \mu^h}{\partial p_j} = N_j^h$$

$$\frac{\partial \boldsymbol{\Delta}_k^h}{\partial p_j} = M_k^{h,j}$$

Solving the linearized problem at $\bar{p}$ is equivalent to finding vectors N^h and matrices M^h that satisfy these relations, plus the equations expressing that μ^h and Δ^h remain on the manifold $\mathcal{M}$ (the latter are obtained by differentiating the equations for $\mathcal{M}$, namely Equation (5.17)). In addition, we want the V^h to be convex.

Formally, we need the following conditions:

- $\boldsymbol{\Delta}^h$ is the gradient of a convex function:

  $$M^h \text{ is symmetric and positive definite, } h = 1, \ldots, n$$

- 'the point remains on the manifold', which leads to:

  $$\begin{aligned} D_p x(\bar{p}) &= \sum_h (\boldsymbol{\Delta}^h (D_p \mu^h)^{\mathrm{T}} + \mu^h D_p \boldsymbol{\Delta}^h) \\ &= \sum_h (\boldsymbol{\Delta}^h (N^h)^{\mathrm{T}} + \mu^h M^h) \end{aligned}$$

  $$M^h p + \boldsymbol{\Delta}^h = -\frac{1}{(\bar{\mu}^h)^2} N_h \Leftrightarrow N_h^{\mathrm{T}} = -(\bar{\mu}^h)^2 (p^T M^h + (\boldsymbol{\Delta}^h)^T)$$

  This is the set of linear equations that have to be solved in M^h and N^h.

Is it possible to find vectors N^h and matrices M^h that satisfy the previous conditions? The answer is yes. The technique used in this proof applies not only to the aggregate demand problem, but also to other problems of the same type.

5.2.2.4 Step 4: apply the Cartan-Kähler theorem

The last step in the proof is to show that all points in $\mathcal{M}$ are *ordinary* in the sense of Cartan. This step is crucial in order to go from a solution to the linearized version at each point to a solution to the general, non-linear problem. Formally, this requirement means that the codimension of the space of solutions has to be computed in two different ways and that the final results must agree. (See Subsection 7.3.4).

In the case of market demand, the existence of a solution to the linearized problem (step one above) is in fact a consequence of known results in the literature, due to Sonnenschein (1973b), Diewert (1977) and Mantel (1977). These results, however, are not sufficient for the present purpose, because they do not allow us to check the codimension properties just mentioned. The proof must allow to compute the required dimensions. In other words, it is important to understand that finding *one* particular solution of the linearized problem is not enough. What we need is a characterization of *all* possible solutions to the linearized problem, since we shall have to compute the dimensions of the corresponding spaces. This is of course more difficult than finding one solution. But it is a problem for which the whole apparatus of linear algebra can be used.

5.3 Aggregate Market Demand With Few Agents

We now investigate the problem of disaggregating market demand when there are fewer agents than goods. The framework is precisely the one of the preceding subsection, but this time $H < N$.

When $H \geq N$, as we just saw, *any* map $x(p)$ satisfying the Walras law is (locally) the market demand of an exchange economy with H consumers, each with a known monetary endowment, normalized to 1. When $H < N$, on the other hand, it is to be expected that $x(p)$ should satisfy some necessary conditions to qualify. One is relatively obvious:

Lemma 5.5. Suppose $x(p)$ is the market demand of an exchange economy with H consumers. Then $x(p)$ must satisfy the SNR$(H-1)$ condition.

Proof. Differentiating formula (5.13), we get:

$$D_p x = -\sum_{h=1}^{H} \frac{1}{\lambda^h} D^2_{pp} V^h + \sum_{h=1}^{H} \frac{1}{(\lambda^h)^2} D_p \lambda^h (DV^h)^{\mathrm{T}}$$

The first term is symmetric, the second term has rank at most H. We can rewrite the expression as follows:

$$\begin{aligned} D_p x = & -\sum_{h=1}^{H} \frac{1}{\lambda^h} D^2_{pp} V^h - \sum_{h=1}^{H} \alpha_h DV^h (DV^h)^{\mathrm{T}} \\ & + \sum_{h=1}^{H} \left(\frac{D_p \lambda^h}{(\lambda^h)^2} + \alpha_h DV^h \right) (DV^h)^{\mathrm{T}} \end{aligned}$$

and, choosing the $\alpha_h > 0$ large enough, the first term now is negative definite. It follows that the Slutsky matrix $S = D_p x(I - px^{\mathrm{T}})$ has the desired property (see Section 3.1.1). □

This condition is the only one which is required; in fact, it is sufficient

---

Theorem 5.6. Let $x(p)$ be an analytic map from some neighborhood of $\bar{p} \in \mathbb{R}^N$ into $\mathbb{R}^N$ satisfying the Walras law $p^T x(p) = H$ and the SNR($H - 1$) condition. Then there is some (possibly smaller) neighborhood of $\bar{p}$ such that $x(p)$ is the market demand of an economy with H agents, each of them with a monetary endowment of 1.

The proof proceeds exactly as in the preceding section, by applying the Cartan–Kähler theorem to the EDS (5.16), but this time the computations are more delicate. Because of condition $SNR(H - 1)$, the 1-form $\omega := \sum x^n(p)dp_n$ satisfies the Darboux condition $\omega \wedge (d\omega)^H = 0$, and this plays a role in verifying the Cartan condition. It also plays a role in finding solutions $V^h, 1 \leq h \leq H$, with $D^2_{pp}V(\bar{p})$ positive definite. We refer to Ekeland and Djitte (2006) for a complete proof.

6

Constraints on Trade and Consumption

6.1 Excess Demand in Incomplete Markets

Section 5 has dealt with complete markets. The market is *incomplete* if certain trades are not possible. Such situations arise naturally in the framework of risk-trading; see for instance Duffie (1992), or MacGill and Quinzii (1997). They are modelled as follows. Denote by $G(K,N)$ the manifold of all K-dimensional linear subspaces of $\mathbb{R}^N$; it is known to have dimension $N(N-K)$. We are given a point $\bar{\theta}$ in a d-dimensional manifold Θ, and a map Φ from some neighborhood $\mathcal{O}$ of $\bar{\theta}$ into $G(K,N)$, so that $\Phi(\theta)$ is a K-dimensional subspace of $\mathbb{R}^N$. We are also given a map z from $\mathcal{O}$ into $\mathbb{R}^N$ such that:

$$z(\theta) \in \Phi(\theta), \quad \forall \theta$$

The disaggregation problem for excess demand consists in finding H concave utility functions U^h and N maps $z_h(\theta)$ such that:

$$\begin{aligned} z(\theta) &= \sum_{h=1}^{H} z_h(\theta) \\ z_h(\theta) &= \text{Arg Max}\ \{U^h(z) \mid z \in \Phi(\theta)\} \end{aligned} \tag{6.1}$$

In the case of complete markets, as described by formula (5.4), we have $\theta = p \in S^{N-1}$, so that $d = N - 1$, and $\Phi(p) = \{z \mid p^{\mathrm{T}} z = 0\}$ has dimension $K = N - 1$. Incomplete markets introduce further restrictions, so that the admissible space $\Phi(\theta)$ has dimension $K < N - 1$. Chiappori and Ekeland (1999c, 2000) have extended to this situation the results in the Sonnenschein, Mantel and Debreu tradition for complete markets: they find that K agents are needed, which is consistent with the result we found for complete markets (bearing in mind that we are dealing with a local result only, so $H = N - 1$ is enough).

Theorem 6.1. Assume that $d \leq N$ and that the maps Φ and z are analytic, with $z(\theta) \in \Phi(\theta)$ in some neighborhood of $\bar{\theta}$. Let there be given H vectors $(\bar{z}_1, \ldots, \bar{z}_H)$ in $\mathbb{R}^N$, with rank at least K and such that:

$$\sum_{h=1}^{H} \bar{z}_h = z(\bar{\theta}) \quad \text{and} \quad \bar{z}_h \in \Phi(\bar{\theta}), \quad h = 1, \ldots, H$$

Then there exists N analytic maps $z_h(\theta)$ defined in some neighborhood of $\bar{\theta}$, with $z_h(\bar{\theta}) = \bar{z}_h$, and for each h an analytic function U^h defined in some neighborhood of $\bar{z}_h$ and concave in that neighborhood, such that Equation (6.1) is satisfied.

We refer to Chiappori and Ekeland (1999c) for a proof, taking into account the correction in Chiappori and Ekeland (2000).

6.2 Individual Demand Under Non-Budgetary Constraints

Individual demand is restricted by the budget constraint. There can also be additional constraints, such as rationing (see Tobin, 1952). In that case, the individual consumer has to solve the following type of problem:

$$\begin{aligned} &\max\nolimits_x U(x) \\ &Px \leq y \end{aligned} \qquad (\mathcal{R})$$

where $x \in \mathbb{R}^N$, P is a $K \times N$ matrix of rank $K < N$, and $y \in \mathbb{R}^K$. It is assumed that the coefficients p_n^k of P are positive, as well as the components y^k of y. This general formulation covers several situations:

the case of monetary endowments, where the constraint is $p^{\mathrm{T}} x \leq 1$; the case of real endowments, where the constraint is $p^{\mathrm{T}} x \leq p^{\mathrm{T}} \omega$; and the case of incomplete markets.

Denote by $x(P, y)$ the solution of problem $(\mathcal{R})$: it is the constrained demand of consumer. Is there an analogue of the Slutsky relations? In other words, given a map $(P, y) \longmapsto x(P, y)$ from $\mathbb{R}^{KN+K}$ into $\mathbb{R}^N$, when does there exist a strictly concave utility function $U(x)$ for which it is the constrained demand? This question has been investigated by Diamond and Yaari (1972) and Epstein (1981) in some special cases, and by Aloqeili (2004) in the general case, using the tools of exterior differential calculus. We will now review these results.

The first observation is that there is a Slutsky matrix for every constraint, and that these Slutsky matrices are all proportional. To see this, denote by $\lambda_k \geq 0$ the Lagrange multiplier associated with the kth constraint, so that:

$$D_p U + \sum_k \lambda_k (y^k - p_n^k x^n) = 0$$

Lemma 6.2. Let $x(P, y)$ be the constrained demand of the consumer and $\lambda_k(P, p), 1 \leq k \leq K$ the corresponding Lagrange multipliers. Set:

$$S_k^{n'n} := \frac{\partial x^{n'}}{\partial p_n^k} + \frac{\partial x^{n'}}{\partial y^k} x^n \tag{6.2}$$

Then:

$$\lambda_k S_{k'}^{nn'} = \lambda_{k'} S_k^{n'n} \quad \forall k, k', n, n'$$

Taking $k = k'$ in these relations, we get $S_k^{nn'} = S_k^{n'n}$, which means that the Slutsky matrix S_k corresponding to the kth constraint is symmetric.

The integrability conditions are quite complicated in the general case (see Aloqueili, 2004). We will write them in the case when $K = 2$, so that there is just one additional constraint. In that case, there are only two Lagrange multipliers, λ_1 and λ_2. We set $\lambda := \lambda_1 / \lambda_2$, and we define the Slutsky matrices S_1 and S_2 by (6.2) with $k = 1, 2$.

Theorem 6.3. Assume that $x(P,y)$ is a constrained demand function. Then there is a scalar function $\lambda(P,y) > 0$ such that λ, S_1 and S_2 satisfy the following relations:

$$S_1 = S_1^{\mathrm{T}}, \quad S_2 = S_2^{\mathrm{T}}, S_1 = \lambda S_2$$

$$\frac{\partial \lambda}{\partial p_n^1} + \frac{\partial \lambda}{\partial y^1} x^n = \lambda \frac{\partial x^n}{\partial y^1} - \frac{\partial x^n}{\partial y^2}, \quad \forall n$$

$$\frac{\partial \lambda}{\partial p_n^2} + \frac{\partial \lambda}{\partial y^2} x^n = \lambda \left(\lambda \frac{\partial x^n}{\partial y^1} - \frac{\partial x^n}{\partial y^2} \right), \quad \forall n$$

and the matrices S_1 and S_2 are negative semi-definite. Conversely, if $x(P,y)$ is a smooth function satisfying the Walras law $Px(P,y) = y$ and the preceding conditions in some neighborhood of $(\bar{P},\bar{y})$, then there exists functions $V(P,y), \lambda_1(P,y) > 0$ and $\lambda_2(P,y) > 0$ on a possibly smaller neighborhood $\mathcal{O}$ such that:

$$dV = -\lambda_1 \left(\sum_{n=1}^{N} x^n dp_n^1 - dy^1 \right) - \lambda_2 \left(\sum_{n=1}^{N} x^n dp_n^2 - dy^2 \right)$$

In addition, $D^2V(P,y)$ is positive semi-definite over the space:

$$E(P,y) := \left\{ (\pi,\eta) \mid (D_{p^i}V)\pi^i + \eta^i \frac{\partial V}{\partial y^i} = 0, \quad i = 1,2 \right\}$$

Note that this falls just short of solving the disaggregation problem. Indeed, the function:

$$U(x) := \min_{(P,y)\in\mathcal{O}} \{V(P,y) \mid Px = y\} \tag{6.3}$$

is the natural candidate for the utility function in problem $(\mathcal{R})$, for, with this choice of $U(x)$, the given function $x(P,y)$ satisfies the first-order conditions for optimality in problem $(\mathcal{R})$, so that the mathematical integration problem is solved. However, it is not clear that the function U defined by (6.3) is quasi-concave, so that it may not be a bona fide utility function (even though the max in problem $(\mathcal{R})$ is attained at a unique point)

7

A User's Guide to Exterior Differential Calculus

In this section, we give a brief but self-contained account of exterior differential calculus (EDC). This is a mathematical tool which was developed in the early twentieth century to solve problems in group theory and geometry, but it recently turned out to be extremely useful for solving problems in the economic theory of demand, as the reader of this book is probably aware by now.

The main contributor to EDC was the French mathematician Elie Cartan (1869–1951), whose book "*Les systèmes différentiels extérieurs et leurs applications géométriques*" (1945) remained for a long time the main reference on the subject. Cartan's early work was generalized and simplified by Erich Kähler (1906–2000) in a very influential booklet "*Einführung in die Theorie der Systeme von Differentialgleichungen*" (1934), where what is now called the Cartan–Kähler theorem is stated in its definitive form. A modern and complete account of the theory is given in the book "*Exterior differential systems*" by Bryant et al. (1991). Cartan is notoriously difficult to read, Kähler is not much help, the book by Bryant *et al.* is quite ponderous. The present section aims to give a coherent and readable account of the tools in EDC that are useful to the economist, and does not intend to provide proofs.

EDC consists of two operations: a purely algebraic one, the exterior product (also called the wedge product, and denoted by $\wedge$, and special kind of differentiation, called the exterior derivative, and denoted by d. They operate on differential forms, which are classified by their degrees: differential forms of degree 0 are just functions, differential forms of degree 1 are analogous to vector fields, and differential forms of degree $k \geq 1$ arise from differential forms of lower degree by taking exterior products and/or exterior derivatives. All the machinery of differential forms and EDC is directed towards proving and applying two major theorems: the Darboux theorem and the Cartan–Kähler theorem. We will state both and show how to use them on a few examples.

7.1 Differential Forms

7.1.1 Definition

Denote by $E = \mathbb{R}^N$ the space of goods, with $x = (x^1, \ldots, x^N)$ a goods bundle, and by $E^* = \mathbb{R}^N$ the space of prices, with $p = (p_1, \ldots, p_N)$ a price system. Algebraically speaking, prices operate on goods to yield a number:

$$\langle p, x \rangle := \sum_{n=1}^{N} p_n x^n \tag{7.1}$$

which is the price of the goods bundle x if the prevailing price system is p. We will express this idea by stating that E^* is the *dual* of E, and we will refer to goods bundles x as *vectors* and to price systems p as *covectors*. Traditionally, vector coordinates are indicated by superscripts, $x = (x^n)_{1 \leq n \leq N}$, and covector coordinates are indicated by subscripts, $p = (p_n)_{1 \leq n \leq N}$. One can then verify the correctness of formulas like (7.1) by checking that the summation index n is written twice in the formula, once as a subscript and once as a superscript. On the other hand, when we are dealing with families of vectors indexed by k, $1 \leq k \leq H$, we will write the index as a subscript, as in $[x_1, \ldots, x_H]$, so that the nth coordinate of x_k appears as x_k^n.

Of course, one could take E to be the space of prices and E^* to be the space of goods. This is the dual point of view, and in this book we have used it as well. In this section, we will take E to be the space of goods. Everything, of course, carries over to the dual situation.

We now choose a basis $[e_1,\dots,e_N]$ in E and a basis $[f^1,\dots,f^N]$ in E^*. We choose them to be dual to each other, meaning that:

$$\langle f^i, e_j\rangle = \begin{cases} 0, & \text{if } i \neq j \\ 1, & \text{if } i = j \end{cases}$$

Definition 7.1. A *vector field* on E is a map $x \mapsto \xi(x)$ from E to itself. A *covector field* on E is a map $x \mapsto \omega(x)$ from E to E^*.

Taking coordinates, we write $\xi(x) = (\xi^1(x),\dots,\xi^N(x))$ and $\pi(x) = (\pi_1(x),\dots,\pi_N(x))$. The vector (or covector) field ξ (or π) is called C^k if the all coordinates ξ^k (or π_k) are k times continuously differentiable functions of x. Covector fields operate on vector fields according to the formula:

$$\langle \pi(x), \xi(x)\rangle := \sum_{n=1}^{N} \pi_n(x)\xi^n(x) \tag{7.2}$$

where the right-hand side is no longer a number, but a function of x, which is C^k if π and ξ are C^k.

Example 7.1. Let $f\colon E \longrightarrow \mathbb{R}$ be a C^k function, $k \geq 1$. Then:

$$df(x) := \left(\frac{\partial f}{\partial x^1}(x),\dots,\frac{\partial f}{\partial x^N}(x)\right) \tag{7.3}$$

is a C^{k-1} covector field. If $\varphi\colon(-\varepsilon,\varepsilon) \longrightarrow E$ is a C^1 curve in E, such that $\varphi(0) = \bar{x}$, then:

$$\frac{d}{dt} f(\varphi(t)) = \sum_{n=1}^{N} \frac{\partial f}{\partial x^n}(\bar{x}) \frac{\partial \varphi^n}{\partial t}(0) \tag{7.4}$$

$$= \langle df(\bar{x}), \varphi'(0)\rangle \tag{7.5}$$

Formula (7.5) makes it very clear that $df(x)$ is a covector field, not a vector field: at the point $\bar{x}$, we define a vector $\varphi'(0)$ which is tangent to a curve $\varphi(t)$ going through $\bar{x}$, and $df(\bar{x})$ operates on that vector.

This distinction is crucial, because one is tempted to view $df(x)$ as a vector field, namely the "gradient vector field" associated with the function f. This is possible, but then one must interpret the right-hand side of formula (7.4) as a scalar product, and this not flexible enough for our purposes. For instance, the basis $(e_1,\ldots,e_N)$ in E would then have to be orthonormal, and we would be limited to changes of coordinates that preserve this property.[1] EDC is valid in any coordinate system, and this is why we stick to the interpretation of $df(x)$ as a covector: it is the price to pay for generality and simplicity.

Definition 7.2. A *differential form of degree* 0 on E is a function f on E.

A *differential form of degree* 1 on E is a covector field π on E.

A *differential form of degree* $H > 1$ (of H-form) on E is a map $\omega\colon E \longmapsto (E^*)^H$, operating on any family $[\xi_1,\ldots,\xi_H]$ of vector fields according to the following rules:

- multilinearity: for any $(\alpha,\beta) \in \mathbb{R}^2$ and any vector field $\zeta(x)$ we have:

$$\begin{aligned}\langle\omega(x),[\alpha\xi_1(x)+\beta\zeta(x),\xi_2(x),\ldots,\xi_H(x)]\rangle \\ = \alpha\langle\omega(x),[\alpha^1(x),\xi_2(x),\ldots,\xi_H(x)]\rangle \\ + \beta\langle\omega(x),[\zeta(x),\xi_2(x),\ldots,\xi_H(x)]\rangle\end{aligned} \tag{7.6}$$

- antisymmetry: for any permutation σ of the indices:

$$\begin{aligned}\langle\omega(x),[\xi_{\sigma(1)}(x),\xi_{\sigma(2)}(x),\ldots,\xi_{\sigma(H)}(x)]\rangle \\ = (-1)^{\text{sign}(\sigma)}\langle\omega(x),[\xi_1(x),\xi_2(x),\ldots,\xi_H(x)]\rangle\end{aligned} \tag{7.7}$$

Here $\text{sign}(\sigma)$ denotes the signature of the permutation: it is either $+1$ or -1, it is $+1$ for the identity, it is -1 if the permutation consists only of interchanging two elements, and if one performs two permutations in succession, the signature of the resulting permutation is the product

[1] These changes of coordinates are given by $x = My$, where the matrix M is orthogonal: $M^*M = I = MM^*$.

of the signatures. This is enough to determine the signature of any permutation.

Note that, because of the antisymmetry, property (7.6) holds, not only for ξ_1, but also for any $\xi_k, 1 \leq k \leq H$.

The basic example of H-form is provided by the exterior product of H forms of degree 1:

Definition 7.3. Let $\pi^1, \ldots, \pi^H$ be 1-forms. Their *exterior product* is denoted by $\pi^1 \wedge \cdots \wedge \pi^H$ and defined as follows:

$$\begin{aligned} &\langle \pi^1(x) \wedge \cdots \wedge \pi^H(x), [\xi_1(x), \xi_2(x), \ldots, \xi_H(x)] \rangle \\ &:= \frac{1}{H!} \sum_\sigma (-1)^{\text{sign}(\sigma)} \Pi_{k=1}^H \langle \pi^k(x), \xi_{\sigma(k)}(x) \rangle \end{aligned} \tag{7.8}$$

The sum is extended over all permutations σ of $\{1, \ldots, H\}$, which number $H!$, hence the normalizing factor on the right-hand side. For instance, taking $H = 2$, we get:

$$\langle \pi^1 \wedge \pi^2, [\xi_1, \xi_2] \rangle = \frac{1}{2}(\langle \pi^1, \xi_1 \rangle \langle \pi^2, \xi_2 \rangle - \langle \pi^1, \xi_2 \rangle \langle \pi^2, \xi_1 \rangle) \tag{7.9}$$

This is clearly bilinear and antisymmetric in ξ_1 and ξ_2, so it is a 2-form. More generally, the right-hand side of formula (7.8) is multilinear and antisymmetric in $\xi_1, \ldots, \xi_H$, so the exterior product $\pi_1 \wedge \cdots \wedge \pi_H$ is an H-form.

Note finally that the exterior product is antisymmetric:

$$\pi_1 \wedge \cdots \wedge \pi_H = (-1)^{\text{sign}(\sigma)} \pi_{\sigma(1)} \wedge \cdots \wedge \pi_{\sigma(H)}$$

As a particular case of this, we have:

$$\pi_1 \wedge \pi_2 = -\pi_2 \wedge \pi_1$$
$$\pi \wedge \pi = 0, \quad \forall \pi$$

There is a kind of converse to this last identity. It is called the *Cartan lemma*:

Proposition 7.2. Consider a family of 1-forms $\alpha^k, \beta^k, 1 \leq k \leq H$, with the α^k linearly independent. Then:

$$\sum_{k=1}^H \alpha^k \wedge \beta^k = 0$$

if and only if there is family of functions $c_{ij}, 1 \leq i, j \leq H$, with $c_{ij} = c_{ji}$, such that $\beta^k = \sum_{i=1}^{H} c_{ik}\alpha_i$.

Proof. The sufficiency part is clear. Substituting the expression for β^k, we get:

$$\begin{aligned}\sum \alpha^k \wedge \beta^k &= \sum \alpha^k \wedge \sum c_{ik}\alpha_i \\ &= \sum_{k<i} (c_{ik} - c_{ki})\alpha^k \wedge \alpha_i = 0\end{aligned}$$

For the converse, choose 1-forms γ_k such that $(\alpha^1(x), \ldots, \alpha^k(x), \gamma_{H+1}(x), \ldots, \gamma_N(x))$ form a basis of the space of covectors for every x, and write:

$$\beta^k = \sum_{i=1}^{H} c_{ik}\alpha_i + \sum_{j=H+1}^{N} m_{jk}\gamma_j$$

Then:

$$\sum_{k=1}^{H} \alpha^k \wedge \beta^k = \sum_{k<i} (c_{ik} - c_{ki})\alpha^k \wedge \alpha_i + \sum_{i,j} c_{ik}m_{jk}\alpha_i \wedge \gamma_j \tag{7.10}$$

Suppose the left-hand side is 0. Consider a vector $\xi_1(x)$ such that $\langle \xi_1(x), \alpha^1(x) \rangle = 1$ while:

$$\langle \xi_1(x), \alpha_i(x) \rangle = \langle \xi_1(x), \gamma_j(x) \rangle = 0, \quad \text{for } 2 \leq i \leq H, H+1 \leq j \leq N$$

and a vector $\zeta_H(x)$ such that $\langle \zeta_H(x), \gamma_{H+1}(x) \rangle = 1$ while:

$$\langle \xi_1(x), \alpha_i(x) \rangle = \langle \xi_1(x), \gamma_j(x) \rangle = 0, \quad \text{for } 1 \leq i \leq H, H+2 \leq j \leq N$$

Substituting the above in Equation (7.10), we get $m_{1,H+1} = 0$. In the same way, we find that all the m_{jk} vanish. We are left with a linear combination of the $\alpha^k \wedge \alpha_i, i < k$, and the same methods show that the coefficients must vanish, so $c_{ik} - c_{ki}$ for all i, k. □

7.1.2 Local Coordinates

We can use these results to write differential forms in a very convenient manner. For this, we first need to define local coordinate systems.

Definition 7.4. Given a point $\bar{x} \in \mathbb{R}^N$ and a C^1 map $\varphi: \Omega \longrightarrow \mathbb{R}^N$, where Ω is some neighborhood of $\bar{x}$, we shall say that $\varphi = (\varphi^1, \dots, \varphi^N)$ is a *local coordinate system* near $\bar{x}$ if $\varphi(\bar{x}) = 0$ and the matrix:

$$D\varphi(\bar{x}) := \left[\frac{\partial \varphi^i}{\partial x^j}(\bar{x})\right]_{1 \le i,j \le N}$$

is invertible.

By the inverse function theorem and the above definition, if $(\varphi^1, \dots, \varphi^N)$ is a local coordinate system near $\bar{x}$, then there is a neighborhood $\Omega' \subset \Omega$ of $\bar{x}$ and a neighborhood $\mathcal{O}$ of 0 in $\mathbb{R}^N$ such that φ maps Ω' onto $\mathcal{O}$ and is invertible; denote by $\psi = (\psi^1, \dots, \psi^N)$ its inverse. Then the equations

$$y^n = \varphi^n(x^1, \dots, x^N), \quad 1 \le n \le N \tag{7.11}$$

and

$$x^n = \psi^n(y^1, .., y^N), \quad 1 \le n \le N \tag{7.12}$$

are equivalent. So any point $x \in \Omega'$ is uniquely defined by the values of $(y^1, \dots, y^N)$ as well as by the values of $(x^1, \dots, x^N)$. In other words, $(y^1, \dots, y^N)$ is another coordinate system for x: it is non-linear, because the defining Equations (7.11) and (7.12) are non-linear, and it is local, because it is valid only in some neighborhood of $\bar{x}$. The basic formulas of EDC will be valid in any such coordinate system.

Of course, if we define a subset $\mathcal{M}$ of $\mathbb{R}^N$ by a system of linear equations in the coordinates $(x^1, \dots, x^N)$, they will no longer be linear in the $(y^1, \dots, y^N)$ coordinates. So $\mathcal{M}$ will no longer be a linear subspace in the $(y^1, \dots, y^N)$ coordinates, but it will retain some regularity properties; for instance, it will have a tangent space at every point. This is expressed in the following definition:

Definition 7.5. A subset $\mathcal{M}$ of $\mathbb{R}^N$ is a *submanifold* of dimension H if, for every $\bar{x} \in \mathcal{M}$, there is a local coordinate system $\varphi: \Omega \longrightarrow \mathbb{R}^N$ near $\bar{x}$ such that:

$$\mathcal{M} \cap \Omega = \{x \mid \varphi^1(x) = \cdots = \varphi^H(x) = 0\}$$

In other words, in the new coordinates $y = \varphi(x)$, $\mathcal{M}$ is defined by the equations $y^1 = \cdots = y^H = 0$.

Pick a (possibly local and non-linear) coordinate system $(x^1, \ldots, x^N)$. For every n, the projection $x \longmapsto x^n$ is a C^∞ function, and by formula (4.3) there is a corresponding 1-form dx^n, defined by:

$$\langle dx^n, \xi(x) \rangle = \xi^n(x) \tag{7.13}$$

Proposition 7.3. Any 1-form can be expressed as a linear combination of the $dx^n, 1 \leq n \leq N$.

Proof. Take any 1-form π. Comparing formulas (7.2) and (7.13), we find that:

$$\langle \pi(x), \xi(x) \rangle = \sum_{n=1}^{N} \pi_n(x) \xi^n(x) = \left\langle \sum_{n=1}^{N} \pi_n(x) dx^n, \xi(x) \right\rangle$$

for any vector field $\xi(x)$. It follows that $\pi = \sum \pi_n dx^n$. □

Formula (7.9) for the exterior product of two 1-forms becomes:

$$\langle dx^i \wedge dx^j, [\xi_1, \xi_2] \rangle = \frac{1}{2} (\xi_1^i(x) \xi_2^j(x) - \xi_1^j(x) \xi_2^i(x)) \tag{7.14}$$

Proposition 7.4. Any 2-form can be expressed as a linear combination of the $dx^i \wedge dx^j, 1 \leq i, j \leq N$.

Proof. Take any 2-form ω. For $1 \leq n \leq N$, consider the vector field $\xi_n(x)$ defined by:

$$\xi_n^i(x) = \begin{pmatrix} 0, & \text{if } i \neq n \\ 1, & \text{if } i = n \end{pmatrix}$$

For $1 < i \neq j < N$, apply ω to the two vector fields ξ_i and ξ_j, and denote the resulting function by ω_{ij}

$$\langle \omega, [\xi_i, \xi_j] \rangle = \omega_{ij}(x)$$

Using the multilinearity and the antisymmetry, one checks that for any two vector field $\xi(x)$ and $\zeta(x)$, we have:

$$\langle \omega, [\xi, \zeta] \rangle = \sum_{i \neq j} \omega_{ij}(x)(\xi^i(x)\zeta^j(x) - \xi^j(x)\zeta^i(x))$$

Comparing with formula (7.14), we get:

$$\langle \omega, [\xi, \zeta] \rangle = \left\langle \sum_{i \neq j} \omega_{ij} dx^i \wedge dx^j, [\xi, \zeta] \right\rangle$$

so that

$$\omega = \sum \omega_{ij} dx^i \wedge dx^j = 2 \sum_{i<j} \omega_{ij} dx^i \wedge dx^j. \qquad \square$$

More generally, one proves that any H-form ω can be expressed as a linear combination of exterior products:

$$\omega(x) = \sum \omega_{n_1 n_2 \cdots n_H}(x) dx^{n_1} \wedge dx^{n_2} \wedge \cdots \wedge dx^{n_H} \tag{7.15}$$

$$= k! \sum_{n_1 < \cdots < n_H} \omega_{n_1 n_2 \cdots n_H}(x) dx^{n_1} \wedge dx^{n_2} \wedge \cdots \wedge dx^{n_H} \tag{7.16}$$

These expressions of general H-forms in terms of exterior products of the 1-forms $dx^1, \ldots, dx^N$ greatly facilitate the manipulation and understanding of differential forms. We derive some immediate consequences.

Proposition 7.5. Set $\omega = \pi^1 \wedge \cdots \wedge \pi^H$, where the $\pi^k(x) = \sum \pi_n^k(x) dx^n$ are 1-forms. Then:

$$\omega = \sum_{n_1 < \cdots < n_H} H! \omega_{n_1 \cdots n_H} dx^{n_1} \wedge \cdots \wedge dx^{n_H}$$

where the coefficients $\omega_{n_1 \cdots n_H}(x) =$ are the $H \times H$ minors of the $H \times N$ matrix $(\pi_j^k(x))_{1 \leq j \leq N}^{1 \leq k \leq H}$

Proof. It is a straightforward computation $\square$

Corollary 7.1. If $\pi^1(x) \wedge \cdots \wedge \pi^H(x) = 0$, then the covectors $\pi^k(x)$ are linearly dependent.

Proof. If all the 2×2 minors vanish, then the matrix has rank 1 or less, so its columns must be collinear. □

More generally, one proves that the coefficients $\omega_{n_1 n_2 \cdots n_H}$ of $\omega = \pi_1 \wedge \cdots \wedge \pi_H$ are the $H \times H$ minors of the $H \times N$ matrix:

$$\Pi(x) := \left(\pi_j^k(x)\right)_{1 \le j \le N}^{1 \le k \le H}$$

If the exterior product $\omega(x)$ vanishes at x, then this matrix has rank less than H, so that its columns $\pi_k(x)$ cannot be linearly independent.

Let us single out the case $H = N$:

Proposition 7.6. Set $\omega = \pi^1 \wedge \cdots \wedge \pi^N$. Then $\omega(x) = \det P(x) dx^1 \wedge \cdots \wedge dx^N$.

As another consequence of the decomposition formulas (7.15) or (7.16), note that all differential forms of degree $H > N$ are identically zero. Indeed, in any exterior product of $H > N$ copies of $dx^1, \ldots, dx^N$, the same index must occur twice, and the product then vanishes.

Finally, these formulas allow us to extend exterior products beyond 1-forms. The exterior product of an H-form α by an L-form β is an $(H + L)$-form $\alpha \wedge \beta$ which is defined as follows:

$$\alpha = \sum \alpha_{n_1 \cdots n_H} dx^{n_1} \wedge \cdots \wedge dx^{n_H}$$

$$\beta = \sum \beta_{m_1 \cdots m_L} dx^{m_1} \wedge \cdots \wedge dx^{m_L}$$

$$\alpha \wedge \beta = \sum \alpha_{n_1 \cdots n_H} \beta_{m_1 \cdots m_L} dx^{n_1} \wedge \cdots \wedge dx^{n_H} \wedge dx^{m_1} \wedge \cdots \wedge dx^{m_L}$$

Note that:

$$\alpha \wedge \beta = (-1)^{HL} \beta \wedge \alpha$$

In particular, $\alpha \wedge \alpha = 0$ if H is odd, for instance when α is a 1-form, but not if H is even.

7.1.3 Exterior Derivative

The last tool of EDC that we have to define is *exterior differentiation.* It is a linear map which associates with every differential form ω of degree H a differential form $d\omega$ of degree $H+1$. It is defined as follows:

- If f is a 0-form (that is, a function), then df is the 1-form that was defined in formula (7.3), namely:

$$df = \sum \frac{\partial f}{\partial x^n} dx^n \tag{7.17}$$

- If $\omega = \sum \omega_{n_1 \cdots n_H} dx_{n_1} \wedge \cdots \wedge dx_{n_H}$ is an H-form, then $d\omega$ is the $(H+1)$-form given by:

$$d\omega = \sum (d\omega_{n_1 \cdots n_H}) \wedge dx_{n_1} \wedge \cdots \wedge dx_{n_H} \tag{7.18}$$

Let us for instance apply this rule to equation (7.17). We get:

$$\begin{aligned} d(df) &= \sum_i d\left(\frac{\partial f}{\partial x^i}\right) \wedge dx^i = \sum_i \left(\sum_j \frac{\partial^2 f}{\partial x^i \partial x^j} dx^j\right) \wedge dx^i \\ &= \sum_{i<j} \left(\frac{\partial^2 f}{\partial x^i \partial x^j} - \frac{\partial^2 f}{\partial x^j \partial x^i}\right) dx^i \wedge dx^j = 0 \end{aligned}$$

Applying this in turn to formula (7.18), we get the fundamental and remarkable property of exterior differentiation:

Proposition 7.7. For every differential form ω, we have:

$$d(d\omega) = 0$$

The converse is known as Poincaré's lemma:

Proposition 7.8. Suppose ω is an H-form satisfying $d\omega = 0$ on a convex set $\mathcal{O}$. Then there is an $(H-1)$-form Ω such that $\omega = d\Omega$ on $\mathcal{O}$.

We can also deduce from formula (7.18) the following:

Proposition 7.9. Let α and β be two differential forms of degree H and L. Then:

$$d(\alpha \wedge \beta) = (d\alpha) \wedge \beta + (-1)^{HL} \alpha \wedge d\beta$$

Another crucial property of exterior differentiation is that it behaves well with respect to changes of variables. Let $\omega = \sum \omega_n dx^n$ be a 1-form, and set $x = \varphi(y)$, where $y = (y^1, \dots, y^P)$ is another set of variables. The 1-form obtained by substituting the variables y^p for the variables x^n is called the *pullback* of ω and denoted by $\varphi^* \omega$. It is given by:

$$\varphi^* \omega := \sum_{n=1}^{N} \omega_n(\varphi(y)) d\varphi^n = \sum_{n=1}^{N} \omega_n(\varphi(y)) \sum_{p=1}^{P} \frac{\partial \varphi^n}{dy^p} dy^p \tag{7.19}$$

$$= \sum_{p=1}^{P} \left(\sum_{n=1}^{N} \omega_n(\varphi(y)) \frac{\partial \varphi^n}{dy^p} \right) dy^p \tag{7.20}$$

We define in a similar way the pullback $\varphi^* \omega$ of any differential form. The next results follow from the definition by a simple calculation:

Proposition 7.10. For any differential forms α and ω, we have:

$$\varphi^*(\alpha \wedge \omega) = (\varphi^* \alpha) \wedge (\varphi^* \omega)$$
$$\varphi^*(d\omega) = d(\varphi^*(\omega))$$

So the two major operations in EDC, the exterior product and the exterior derivative, commute with pullbacks. In other words, computations are coordinate-independent: we go from one set of coordinates to another by simply replacing ω with $\varphi^* \omega$ in all EDC formulas. Of course, computations are greatly facilitated by the fact that $dd = 0$: there are no higher-order derivatives in EDC. At first glance, this may seem a tremendous loss of information. In fact, it is the greatest asset of EDC: it automatically cuts out coordinate-dependent information. For instance, if we change variables, setting $x = \varphi(y)$, and we seek to express the second derivative of a function $f(x)$ in the new coordinates, we get:

$$\frac{\partial^2}{\partial y^i \partial y^i}[f(\varphi(y))] = \sum_{n,m} \frac{\partial^2 f}{\partial x^n \partial x^m}(\varphi(x)) \frac{\partial \varphi^n}{\partial y^i} \frac{\partial \varphi^m}{\partial y^j}$$
$$+ \sum_{n} \frac{\partial f}{\partial x^n}(\varphi(x)) \frac{\partial^2 \varphi^n}{\partial y^i \partial y^j}, \quad 1 \le i, j \le n$$

The reader will check that, depending on the values of $\partial^2\varphi^n/\partial y^i\partial y^j$, $1 \le i, j, n \le N$, the right-hand side can be any symmetric matrix. Suppose for instance $f(x)$ is convex, so $\partial^2 f/\partial y^i \partial y^j$ is positive definite; then the first term on the right-hand side will be positive definite, but not the second, so there is no reason why $f(\varphi(x))$ should be convex. So convexity is coordinate-dependent,[2] and EDC automatically cuts out that information. The only property that is preserved is symmetry: in the new coordinates as well as in the old ones, the matrix of second derivatives is symmetric, and this is precisely what is expressed by $dd = 0$.

7.2 Frobenius, Darboux and All That

In this section, we will address two questions:

Question 1: Given a 1-form $\omega(x)$ on $\mathbb{R}^N$, and a number H, when can we find functions $V^k(x)$ and $\lambda_k(x)$, $1 \le k \le H$, such that:

$$\omega = \sum_{k=1}^{H} \lambda_k dV^k \tag{7.21}$$

Finding the V_k and μ_k is known as *mathematical integration.*

Question 2: In the decomposition (7.21), can we take the $\lambda_k(x)$ to be positive and the $V^k(x)$ to be convex?

This is known in the literature as *economic integration.*

All statements in this section are local. That is, in each case, it is understood (but not explicitly stated, to avoid tedious repetitions) that the assumptions hold in an open neigborhood of some point $\bar{x}$, and that the conclusion will then hold in a (perhaps smaller) neighborhood of the same point.

7.2.1 The Frobenius Theorem

Consider a family $\alpha^h, 1 \le h \le H$, of 1-forms, defined on some open subset $\mathcal{O} \subset \mathbb{R}^N$, such that the $\alpha^h(x)$ are linearly independent for all $x \in \mathcal{O}$.

[2] Except, of course, if one restricts oneself to linear changes of coordinates, which is not the case in EDC.

We shall denote by $E(x)$ their linear span:

$$E = \mathrm{Span}\{\alpha^1, \ldots, \alpha^H \mid 1 \leq k \leq H\}$$

Let us write down explicitly what this formula means: a 1-form ω belongs to if and only if, for each $x \in \mathcal{O}$, $\omega(x)$ can be expressed as a linear combination of 1-forms in $\mathcal{O}$:

$$\omega(x) = \sum_{h=1}^{H} \mu_h(x)\alpha^h(x)$$

The coefficients $\mu_h(x)$ are then automatically smooth functions of x. We shall say that the $\alpha^h, 1 \leq h \leq H$, *generate* the space E. Of course, there are very many families which generate the same space E. We now ask whether there is one consisting only of exterior derivatives dV^h :

Question 3: When can we find functions $V^h(x), 1 \leq h \leq H$, such that the dV^h generate E ?

$$\mathrm{Span}\{\alpha^1, \ldots, \alpha^H\} = E = \mathrm{Span}\{dV^1, \ldots, dV^H\} \tag{7.22}$$

Definition 7.6. $E = \mathrm{Span}\{\alpha^1, \ldots, \alpha^H\}$ is *closed under differentiation* (or simply *closed*) if, for every h, there are 1-forms $\sigma_i^h, 1 \leq i \leq H$ such that:

$$d\alpha^h = \sum_{i=1}^{H} \sigma_i^h \wedge \alpha^i, \quad \text{for } h = 1, \ldots, H \tag{7.23}$$

For this definition to make sense, we have to show that it does not depend on the particular basis $\{\alpha^h\}$ chosen for E. Indeed, pick another one $\{\beta^h\}$. We then have $\beta^h = \sum_j \mu_j^h \alpha^j$ and $\alpha^i = \sum_s \lambda_s^i \beta^s$. Differentiating, we get:

$$\begin{aligned}
d\beta^h &= \sum_j \mu_j^h \wedge d\alpha^j + \sum_i d\mu_j^h \wedge \alpha^j \\
&= \sum_{j,i} (\mu_j^h \wedge \sigma_i^j + d\mu_i^h) \wedge \alpha^i \\
&= \sum_{i=1}^{H} \left(\sum_{j,s=1}^{H} \lambda_i^s (\mu_j^h \wedge \sigma_s^j + d\mu_s^h) \right) \wedge \beta^i
\end{aligned}$$

which is similar to formula (7.23), with σ_{hi} replaced with $\sum_{j,s=1}^{H}\sum_{j,s=1}^{H}\lambda_i^s(\mu_j^h \wedge \sigma_s^j + d\mu_s^h)$.

Note that the closedness condition (7.23) can also be written in the following way:

$$d\alpha^h \wedge \alpha^1 \wedge \cdots \wedge \alpha^H = 0, \quad \text{for } h = 1, \ldots, H \tag{7.24}$$

Theorem 7.11. (Frobenius) Suppose $E = \text{Span}\{\alpha^1, \ldots, \alpha^H\}$ is generated by a family $\{dV^1, \ldots, dV^H\}$. Then E is closed under differentiation. Conversely, if $E = \text{Span}\{\alpha^1, \ldots, \alpha^H\}$ is closed under differentiation, then there are functions $V^1, \ldots, V^H$ such that $E = \text{Span}\{dV^1, \ldots, dV^H\}$:

$$\omega \in E \Longrightarrow \omega(x) = \sum_{h=1}^{H} \lambda_h(x) dV^h(x) \tag{7.25}$$

Proof. The first part is easy. If $E = \text{Span}\{dV^1, \ldots, dV^H\}$, then $d(dV^h) = 0$, so condition (7.23) is obviously satisfied, and E is closed under differentiation. The converse is more delicate, and proceeds by induction on H, starting with $H = N - 1$ (which reduces to an ordinary differential equation) and working downwards; we refer to Bryant et al. (1991, pp. 27–30), for a complete proof. □

Since the dV^h are linearly independent, we can choose a local coordinate system $(x^1, \ldots, x^N)$ such that $x^h = V^h$ for $1 \le h \le H$. In this coordinate system, condition (7.25) becomes:

$$\omega \in E \Longleftrightarrow \omega(x) = \sum_{h=1}^{H} \omega_h(x^1, \ldots, x^N) dx^h \tag{7.26}$$

In the particular case when $d\omega = 0$, so that $\omega = df$ by the Poincaré lemma, f must be a function of the H first coordinates only. So ω itself must depend only on the H first coordinates:

$$\omega(x) = \sum_{h=1}^{H} \omega_h(x^1, \ldots, x^H) dx^h \tag{7.27}$$

This observation enables us to address the question of the uniqueness of the spanning family $\{dV^1, \ldots, dV^H\}$

Proposition 7.12. Suppose $E = \mathrm{Span}\{dV^1,\ldots,dV^H\} = \mathrm{Span}\{dU^1,\ldots, dU^H\}$. Then there are H functions $\varphi^h : \mathbb{R}^H \longmapsto \mathbb{R}$, such that:

$$U^h = \varphi^h(V^1,\ldots,V^H), \quad 1 \leq h \leq H, s \tag{7.28}$$

Conversely, if $dV^1,\ldots,dV^H$ span E, and $\varphi^1,\ldots,\varphi^H$ are any H functions of H variables, then E is also spanned by the dU^h, where the U^h are given by (7.28).

7.2.2 The First Darboux Theorem

Consider now the case when E is generated by a single 1-form ω:

$$E(x) = \mathbb{R}\omega(x)$$

E is closed under differentiation if and only if ω satisfies one of the two equivalent conditions:

(1) There is a 1-form σ such that $d\omega = \sigma \wedge \omega$
(2) $\omega \wedge d\omega = 0$.

They will be referred to as the *Darboux condition.* The first one comes from (7.23), the second one from (7.24). If they are satisfied, there is a function V such that dV generates E. In particular, ω itself must be collinear to dV: there is a smooth function $\lambda(x)$ such that $\omega = \lambda dV$. More precisely:

Theorem 7.13. Suppose a 1-form ω satisfies:

$$\omega \wedge d\omega = 0 \tag{7.29}$$

Then there is a smooth function λ such that

$$\omega = \lambda dV \tag{7.30}$$

Conversely, if (7.29) holds on an open set $\mathcal{O}$, for some functions $\lambda(x)$ and $V(x)$, then Equation (7.30) holds as well.

Given ω, are λ and V uniquely determined?

Proposition 7.14. Suppose $\omega = \lambda dV = \mu dU$. Then there we have $\mu = \varphi(\lambda, V)$ and $U = \psi(V)$ for some functions φ and ψ.

Proof. Consider the linear space E generated by $d\lambda$ and dV:

$$E = \mathrm{Span}\{d\lambda, dV\}$$

A 1-form α belongs to E if and only if $\alpha \wedge d\lambda \wedge dV = 0$. Since $d\lambda \wedge dV = d\omega$, this can be rewritten as:

$$\alpha \wedge d\omega = \alpha \wedge d\mu \wedge dU = 0$$

and it follows that both $d\mu$ and dU belong to E. By the uniqueness of proposition 7.12, there are two functions of two variables φ and ψ such that $\mu = \varphi(\lambda, V)$ and $U = \psi(\lambda, V)$. Substituting, we get:

$$\lambda dV = \varphi(\lambda, V) \left(\frac{\partial \psi}{\partial \lambda} d\lambda + \frac{\partial \psi}{\partial V} dV \right)$$

so that $(\partial \psi / \partial \lambda = 0$. □

It is instructive to express Theorem 7.13 in local coordinates. Consider a 1-form $\omega(x)$:

$$\omega(x) = \sum \omega_n(x) dx^n$$

We are looking for a pair of functions $\lambda(x)$ and $V(x)$ such that $\omega = \lambda dV$, meaning that:

$$\omega_n(x) = \lambda(x) \frac{\partial V}{\partial x^n}, \quad 1 \leq n \leq N \tag{7.31}$$

Lemma 7.15. The Darboux condition is equivalent to each of the following:

$$\omega_h \left(\frac{\partial \omega_i}{\partial x^j} - \frac{\partial \omega_j}{\partial x^i} \right) + \omega_i \left(\frac{\partial \omega_j}{\partial x^h} - \frac{\partial \omega_h}{\partial x^j} \right) + \omega_j \left(\frac{\partial \omega_h}{\partial x^i} - \frac{\partial \omega_i}{\partial x^h} \right) = 0 \quad \forall i, j, h \tag{7.32}$$

The matrix

$$s_{ij} := \left(\frac{\partial \omega_i}{\partial x^j} - \frac{\partial \omega_j}{\partial x^i} \right) \tag{7.33}$$

has rank 2, and ω belongs to its range.

Proof. Condition (7.32) comes from computing $\omega \wedge d\omega$ in local coordinates. Condition (7.33) comes from writing $d\omega = \sigma \wedge \omega$. We get:

$$s_{ij} = \frac{\partial \omega_i}{\partial x^j} - \frac{\partial \omega_j}{\partial x^i} = \sigma_i \omega_j - \sigma_j \omega_i$$

$S = (s_{ij})$ is clearly an antisymmetric matrix. If $\xi = (\xi^n)$ is orthogonal both to $\sigma = (\sigma_n)$ and to $\omega = (\omega_n)$, then $S\xi = 0$, so the kernel of S has codimension 2 and S has rank 2. Finally, for any vector ξ which is orthogonal to ω, we have:

$$(S\xi)_i = \sum (\sigma_i \omega_j - \sigma_j \omega_i) \xi^j = -\left(\sum \sigma_j \xi^j\right) \omega_i$$

so that ω is in the range of S. We leave the converse to the reader. □

Corollary 7.2. Both (7.32) and (7.33) are necessary and sufficient condition for (7.31) to hold.

7.2.3 Slutsky Symmetry

In this subsection, and in this subsection only, the variables in $\mathbb{R}^N$ will be denoted by $p = (p_1, \ldots, p_N)$, to fit in with the set-up and notation of earlier papers. Slutsky symmetry is the special form that the Darboux condition takes when the 1-form

$$\omega = \sum_{n=1}^{N} x^n(p) dp_n \tag{7.34}$$

satisfies the additional condition:

$$\sum_{n=1}^{N} p_n x^n(p) = 1 \tag{7.35}$$

To find that special form, we introduce the vector field $\pi(p) = (p_1, \ldots, p_N)$, so that condition (7.35) becomes $\langle \omega, \pi \rangle = 1$. Writing this into the Darboux condition $d\omega = \sigma \wedge \omega$, we get:

$$d\omega(\pi, \xi) = \sigma(\pi)\omega(\xi) - \sigma(\xi)\omega(\pi) = \sigma(\pi)\omega(\xi) - \sigma(\xi)$$

which determines σ up to a constant $\sigma(\pi)$. The Darboux condition now becomes:

$$\begin{aligned} d\omega(\xi,\zeta) &= (\sigma \wedge \omega)(\xi,\zeta) = -(d\omega(\pi,\cdot) \wedge \omega)(\xi,\zeta) \\ &= d\omega(\pi,\zeta)\omega(x) - d\omega(\pi,\xi)\omega(\zeta) \end{aligned}$$

We now express $d\omega$ and $d\omega(\pi,\cdot)$ in local coordinates:

$$d\omega = \sum_{i,j} \frac{\partial x^i}{\partial p_j} dp_j \wedge dp_i$$

$$d\omega(\pi,\xi) = \sum_{i,j} \frac{\partial x^i}{\partial p_j} (p_j \xi^i - \xi^j p_i)$$

and we substitute into the Darboux condition. We get, for every ξ and ζ in $\mathbb{R}^N$:

$$\begin{aligned} \sum_{i,j} \left(\frac{\partial x^i}{\partial p_j} - \frac{\partial x^j}{\partial p_i} \right) \xi_i \zeta_j = \sum_{i,j,k} \bigg(& \frac{\partial x^i}{\partial p_k} p_k x^j + \frac{\partial x^k}{\partial p_j} p_k x^i \\ & - \frac{\partial x^j}{\partial p_k} p_k x^i - \frac{\partial x^k}{\partial p_i} p_k x^j \bigg) \xi_i \zeta_j \end{aligned} \tag{7.36}$$

On the other hand, differentiating the identity (7.35) gives:

$$\sum_k \frac{\partial x^k}{\partial p_j} p_k = \frac{\partial}{\partial p_j} \left(\sum_k x^k p_k \right) - \sum_k x^k \frac{\partial p_k}{\partial p_j} = -x^j,$$

so that (7.36) reduces to:

$$\sum_{i,j} \left(\frac{\partial x^i}{\partial p_j} - \frac{\partial x^j}{\partial p_i} \right) \xi_i \zeta_j = \sum_{i,j,k} \left(\frac{\partial x^i}{\partial p_k} p_k x^j - \frac{\partial x_j}{\partial p_k} p_k x^i \right) \xi_i \zeta_j$$

This means that:

$$\frac{\partial x^i}{\partial p_j} - \sum_k \frac{\partial x^i}{\partial p_k} p_k x^j = \frac{\partial x^j}{\partial p_i} - \sum_k \frac{\partial x^j}{\partial p_k} p_k x^i, \quad \text{for all } i,j$$

In other words, the Slutsky matrix is symmetric.

7.2.4 The Second Darboux Theorem

We go back to the standard notations of this section: variables are back to $x = (x^1, \ldots, x^N)$.

Given a 1-form ω, and a number H, we want to know whether there exists H smooth functions $(\lambda_h(x), V^h(x))$ such that:

$$\omega = \sum_{h=1}^{H} \lambda_h(x) dV^h \tag{7.37}$$

If $H \geq N$, this is always possible: it is enough to find N functions $V^n(x), 1 \leq n \leq N$, such that the dV^n are linearly independent. Then every covector, including $\omega(x)$, can be expressed as a linear combination of the dV^n, and the coefficients $\lambda_n(x)$ can easily be shown to be smooth functions of x. So the question really arises when $H < N$. In fact, as the following will show, the decomposition (7.37) is always possible when $H \geq N/2$, so the question really arises when $H < N/2$. For instance, in $\mathbb{R}^3$ and $\mathbb{R}^4$, any 1-form is a linear combination of two derivatives — in another, slightly improper, but more striking, any vector field in $\mathbb{R}^3$ and $\mathbb{R}^4$ is a linear combination of two gradients. This is no longer the case in $\mathbb{R}^5$.

Theorem 7.16. (Darboux) A necessary and sufficient condition for the decomposition (7.37) to hold is that:

$$\omega \wedge (d\omega)^H = 0 \tag{7.38}$$

$$\omega \wedge (d\omega)^{H-1} \neq 0 \tag{7.39}$$

As usual, this is a local result, meaning that the Darboux condition (7.38) is supposed to hold in a neighborhood of some point x, and then the decomposition (4.10) will hold in some (perhaps smaller) neighborhood of the same point. Condition (7.39) means that $\omega \wedge (d\omega)^{H-1}$ should be non-zero at every point in the neighborhood under consideration; it will ensure that the decomposition (7.38) does not hold with $(H-1)$ terms only, and avoid some degenerate cases as well.

It is easy to check that the Darboux condition is necessary. Indeed, if it holds, we have:

$$d\omega = \sum_{h=1}^{H} d\lambda_h \wedge dV^h$$

$$(d\omega)^H = (H!) d\lambda_1 \wedge dV^1 \wedge \cdots \wedge d\lambda_H \wedge dV^H$$

so that $\omega \wedge (d\omega)^H = 0$. In the case when $H = 1$, we already showed that the condition is sufficient, as a direct application of the Frobenius theorem. We refer to Bryant *et al.* (1991, p. 27–30), for the proof in the general case.

Corollary 7.3. If $2H \geq N$, the decomposition (7.37) is always possible

Proof. When $k > N$, any k-form on $\mathbb{R}^N$ is identically zero. So, it $2H \geq N$, the Darboux condition is automatically satisfied. □

As we did in the case $H = 1$, we ask whether the decomposition is unique, and we will connect the Darboux condition to the $SR(H)$ condition which appeared in previous sections. To keep notations at a minimum, we will deal only with the case $H = 2$.

Proposition 7.17. Suppose we have:

$$\omega = \lambda_1 dV^1 + \lambda_2 dV^2 = \mu_1 dU^1 + \mu_2 dU^2 \tag{7.40}$$

and the $dV^1, dV^2, d(\lambda_1/\lambda_2)$ are linearly independent. Then there are two continuous functions F and G such that:

$$U^1 = F\left(V^1, V^2, \frac{\lambda_1}{\lambda_2}\right) \tag{7.41}$$

$$U^2 = G\left(V^1, V^2, \frac{\lambda_1}{\lambda_2}\right) \tag{7.42}$$

The functions $F(t_1, t_2, t_3)$ and $G(t_1, t_2, t_3)$ then satisfy the partial differential equation:

$$\frac{\partial G}{\partial t_1}\frac{\partial F}{\partial t_3} - \frac{\partial G}{\partial t_3}\frac{\partial F}{\partial t_1} = t_3 \left(\frac{\partial G}{\partial t_2}\frac{\partial F}{\partial t_3} - \frac{\partial G}{\partial t_3}\frac{\partial F}{\partial t_2}\right). \tag{7.43}$$

and (μ_1, μ_2) are completely determined by the choice of F and G.

Proof. Let us make some initial computations:

$$d\omega = d\lambda_1 \wedge dV^1 + d\lambda_2 \wedge dV^2$$
$$\omega \wedge d\omega = (\lambda_1 d\lambda_2 - \lambda_2 d\lambda^1) \wedge dV^1 \wedge dV^2$$
$$= -(\lambda_2)^2 d\left(\frac{\lambda_1}{\lambda_2}\right) \wedge dV^1 \wedge dV^2$$
$$d\omega \wedge d\omega = 2\ d\lambda_1 \wedge dV^1 \wedge d\lambda_2 \wedge dV^2$$

Following Ekeland and Nirenberg (2002), we introduce the set E of 1-forms:

$$E = \{\alpha \in E_1 \mid \alpha \wedge \omega \wedge d\omega = 0\}$$

It is clear that $E(x)$ is a linear space. It can be rewritten as:

$$E = \left\{\alpha \in E_1 \mid \alpha \wedge d\left(\frac{\lambda_1}{\lambda_2}\right) \wedge dV^1 \wedge dV^2 = 0\right\}$$

so that $E = \text{Span}\{dV^1, dV^2, d(\lambda_1/\lambda_2)\}$.

Suppose now $\omega = \mu_1 dU^1 + \mu_2 dU^2$. We have, by the same computations as before:

$$\omega \wedge d\omega = -(\mu_2)^2 d\left(\frac{\mu_1}{\mu_2}\right) \wedge dU^1 \wedge dU^2$$

so that $dU^1 \wedge \omega \wedge d\omega = 0$, so that $dU^1 \in E$. From the same argument, it follows that dU^2 and $d(\mu_1/\mu_2)$ belong to E as well. By Proposition 7.12, we have:

$$U^1 = F\left(V^1, V^2, \frac{\lambda_1}{\lambda_2}\right)$$
$$U^2 = G\left(V^1, V^2, \frac{\lambda_1}{\lambda_2}\right)$$
$$\frac{\mu_1}{\mu_2} = H\left(V^1, V^2, \frac{\lambda_1}{\lambda_2}\right)$$

for functions F, G, H. Hence:

$$dU^1 = \frac{\partial F}{\partial t_1} dV^1 + \frac{\partial F}{\partial t_2} dV^2 + \frac{\partial F}{\partial t_3} d\left(\frac{\lambda_1}{\lambda_2}\right)$$
$$dU^2 = \frac{\partial G}{\partial t_1} dV^1 + \frac{\partial G}{\partial t_2} dV^2 + \frac{\partial G}{\partial t_3} d\left(\frac{\lambda_1}{\lambda_2}\right)$$

Substituting in (7.40) we get:

$$\begin{aligned}\omega =& \lambda_1 dV^1 + \lambda_2 dV^2 \\ =& \left(\mu_1 \frac{\partial F}{\partial t_1} + \mu_2 \frac{\partial G}{\partial t_1}\right) dV^1 + \left(\mu_1 \frac{\partial F}{\partial t_2} + \mu_2 \frac{\partial G}{\partial t_2}\right) dV^2 \\ &+ \left(\mu_1 \frac{\partial F}{\partial t_3} + \mu_2 \frac{\partial G}{\partial t_3}\right) d\left(\frac{\lambda_1}{\lambda_2}\right)\end{aligned}$$

Hence:

$$\begin{aligned}\lambda_1 &= \mu_1 \frac{\partial F}{\partial t_1} + \mu_2 \frac{\partial G}{\partial t_1} \\ \lambda_2 &= \mu_1 \frac{\partial F}{\partial t_2} + \mu_2 \frac{\partial G}{\partial t_2} \\ 0 &= \mu_1 \frac{\partial F}{\partial t_3} + \mu_2 \frac{\partial G}{\partial t_3}\end{aligned}$$

This is a system of three linear equations for the two variables (μ_1, μ_2). Since it has a solution, its rank must be 2, and hence Equation (7.43). Once G and F are determined (and hence $U^1$and U^2), μ_1 and μ_2 follow from the decomposition $\omega = \mu_1 \, dU^1 + \mu_2 \, dU^2$. □

7.2.5 Condition SR(H − 1)

We want to express the Darboux condition $\omega \wedge (d\omega)^H = 0$ in local coordinates, as a property of the Slutsky matrix $S(x) = (s_{ij}), 1 \leq i, j \leq N$, associated which ω. In local coordinates $(x^1, \ldots, x^n)$, it is expressed as:

$$s_{ij}(x) = \frac{\partial \omega_i}{\partial x^j} - \omega_j(x) \sum_{n=1}^{N} \frac{\partial \omega_i}{\partial x^n} x^n \tag{7.44}$$

where the 1-form $\omega = \sum_{i=1}^{N} \omega_n(x) dx^n$ is assumed to satisfy the additional condition (Walras law):

$$\sum_{n=1}^{N} \omega_n(x) x^n = 1 \tag{7.45}$$

or, in differentiated form:

$$\sum_{n=1}^{N} \frac{\partial \omega_n}{\partial x^i} x^n + \omega_i(x) = 0, \quad i = 1, \ldots, N \tag{7.46}$$

We first prove an algebraic lemma:

Lemma 7.18. Suppose a 2-form σ on $\mathbb{R}^N$ satisfies $(\sigma)^H = 0$ for some H with $2H \leq N$. Then there are H pairs of 1-forms $\alpha^h, \beta^h, 1 \leq h \leq H$, such that:

$$\sigma = \sum_{h=1}^{H-1} \alpha^h \wedge \beta^h$$

Proof. We proceed by induction on N. For $N = 2$ or 3, the only possibility is $H = 1$, and the result is another way of stating that $\sigma = 0$. Now suppose the result holds up to and including $N - 1$, and take a 2-form σ on $\mathbb{R}^N$ satisfies $(\sigma)^H = 0$, with $2H \leq N$. Take a basis $\{\alpha^1, \ldots, \alpha^N\}$ for the space of 1-forms, and write the 2-form σ in that basis. We get:

$$\begin{aligned}
\sigma &= \sum_{i<j} \sigma_{ij} \alpha^i \wedge \alpha^j \\
&= \alpha^1 \wedge \sum \sigma_{1j} \alpha^j + \sum_{i>1} \alpha^i \wedge \left(\sum_{j>i} \sigma_{ij} \alpha^j \right) \\
&= \alpha^1 \wedge \beta^1 + \sum_{1<i<N} \alpha^i \wedge \beta^i
\end{aligned}$$

where $\beta^h \in \mathrm{Span}\{\alpha^h, \ldots, \alpha^N\}$. We raise both sides to the exterior power H, taking note that all the terms which contain $\alpha^1 \wedge \alpha^1$ must vanish. We get:

$$(\sigma)^H = \left(\sum_{1<i<N} \alpha^i \wedge \beta^i \right)^H + H\alpha^1 \wedge \beta^1 \wedge \left(\sum_{1<i<N} \alpha^i \wedge \beta^i \right)^{H-1} \tag{7.47}$$

Since $(\sigma)^H = 0$, the whole sum vanishes. Applying it to families of vectors $\xi_h, 1 \leq h \leq 2H$, which are orthogonal to α^1, so that $\langle \alpha^1, \xi_h \rangle = 0$, we find that the first term vanishes, so the second one must vanish as well. Applying the second term to families of vectors $\xi_h, 1 \leq h \leq 2H$, such that $< \alpha^1, \xi_h >= 1$ for $h = 1,2$ and $< \alpha^1, \xi_h >= 0$ for $3 \leq h \leq H$, we find that:

$$\left(\sum_{1<i<N} \alpha^i \wedge \beta^i \right)^{H-1} = 0$$

But this is now a 2-form on $\mathbb{R}^{N-1}$ whose $(H-1)$-th exterior power vanishes. Since $2H \leq N$, we have $2(H-1) < N-1$, and the induction assumption applies. This concludes the proof. □

Proposition 7.19. Given H with $2H+1 \leq N$, the following statements about a 1-form ω are equivalent:

(a) The Darboux condition: $\omega \wedge (d\omega)^H = 0$

(b) There exists one-forms $\gamma, \alpha^h, \beta^h$ such that

$$d\omega = \sum_{h=1}^{H-1} \alpha^h \wedge \beta^h + \omega \wedge \gamma \tag{7.48}$$

(c) Condition SR$(H-1)$: the Slutsky matrix $S(x)$ defined by (7.44) decomposes as the sum of a symmetric matrix and a matrix of rank $(H-1)$:

$$s_{ij} = m_{ij} + \sum_{h=1}^{H-1} a_i^h b_j^h, \quad m_{ij} = m_{ji}, \quad i,j = 1,\dots,N \tag{7.49}$$

Proof. If (b) holds, we have:

$$(d\omega)^H = H!(\alpha^1 \wedge \beta^1) \wedge \cdots \wedge (\alpha^{H-1} \wedge \beta^{H-1}) \wedge \omega \wedge \gamma$$

and the Darboux condition follows directly. To prove the converse, we argue as in the preceding lemma, taking a basis $\{\omega, \alpha^2, \dots, \alpha^N\}$ for the space of 1-forms, so that:

$$d\omega = \omega \wedge \gamma + \sum_{n=2}^{N-1} \alpha^n \wedge \beta^n \tag{7.50}$$

where $\beta^h \in \mathrm{Span}\{\alpha^h, \ldots, \alpha^N\}$. We then have:

$$(d\omega)^H = \left(\sum_{n=2}^{N-1} \alpha^n \wedge \beta^n\right)^H + H\omega \wedge \gamma^1 \left(\sum_{n=2}^{N-1} \alpha^n \wedge \beta^n\right)^{H-1}$$

From the Darboux condition, it follows that:

$$\left(\sum_{n=2}^{N-1} \alpha^n \wedge \beta^n\right)^H = 0$$

We have found a 2-form on $\mathbb{R}^{N-1}$ whose Hth exterior power vanishes. Since $2H \leq N - 1$, we can apply Lemma 7.18 to show that the parenthesis can be rearranged to contain exactly $H - 1$ terms. Writing this back into formula (7.50), we find that the Darboux condition implies (a).

Writing condition SR$(H - 1)$ into the definition of $d\omega$, we get:

$$d\omega = \sum_{j<i} \left(\frac{\partial \omega_i}{\partial x^j} - \frac{\partial \omega_j}{\partial x^i}\right) dx^j \wedge dx^i \tag{7.51}$$

$$= \sum_{j<i} \left(s_{ij} - s_{ji} + \sum_h \frac{\partial \omega_i}{\partial x^h} \omega^j(x) x^h - \sum_h \frac{\partial \omega_j}{\partial x^h} \omega^i(x) x^h\right) dx^j \wedge dx^i$$

$$= \sum_{j<i} \left\{\sum_{h=1}^{H-1} (a_i^h b_j^h - a_j^h b_i^h) + \left(\sum_{n=1}^{N} \frac{\partial \omega_i}{\partial x^n} \omega^j x^n - \sum_{n=1}^{N} \frac{\partial \omega_j}{\partial x^n} \omega^i x^n\right)\right\} dx^j \wedge dx^i$$

$$= \sum_{h=1}^{H-1} \sum_{j<i} (a_i^h b_j^h - a_j^h b_i^h) dx^j \wedge dx^i + \omega \wedge \gamma,$$

$$\text{where } \gamma = \sum_{i=1}^{N} \left(\sum_{n=1}^{N} \frac{\partial \omega_i}{\partial x^n} x^n\right) dx^i$$

$$= \sum_{h=1}^{H-1} \beta_h \wedge \alpha_h + \omega \wedge \gamma, \tag{7.52}$$

where $\alpha_h = \sum a_i^h dx^i$ and $\beta_h = \sum b_i^h dx^i$.

So condition SR$(H - 1)$ implies (b). Finally, we prove the converse. Consider the vector field ξ defined by $\xi^n(x) = x^n$. From formulas (7.48) and (7.45), we conclude that:

$$d\omega(\xi,\bullet) = \sum_{h=1}^{H-1} \alpha^h(\xi)\beta^h - \sum \beta^h(\xi)\alpha^h + \gamma - \gamma(\xi)\omega$$

which defines γ in terms of $d\omega(\xi,\bullet)$, the α^h and the $\beta^h, 1 \leq h \leq H-1$. Replacing γ by its value, we get:

$$\begin{aligned} d\omega &= \sum_{h=1}^{H-1} \alpha^h \wedge \beta^h + \omega \wedge \left(d\omega(\xi,\bullet) - \sum_{h=1}^{H-1} \alpha^h(\xi)\beta^h + \sum \beta^h(\xi)\alpha^h + \gamma(\xi)\omega \right) \\ &= \sum_{h=1}^{H-1} (\alpha^h - \alpha^h(\xi)\omega) \wedge (\beta^h - \beta^h(\xi)\omega) + \omega \wedge d\omega(\xi,\bullet) \end{aligned} \quad (7.53)$$

Let us compute the last term. We get:

$$\begin{aligned} d\omega(\xi,\bullet) &= \sum_{i,j} \frac{\partial \omega_i}{\partial x^j}(x^j dx^i - x^i dx^j) \\ &= \sum_{i,j} \frac{\partial \omega_i}{\partial x^j} x^j dx^i + \sum_j \omega^j dx^j \\ &= \sum_{i,j} \frac{\partial \omega_i}{\partial x^j} x^j dx^i + \omega \end{aligned}$$

where relation (7.46) has been used. Substituting in formula (7.53) yields finally:

$$d\omega = \sum_{h=1}^{H-1} (\alpha^h - \alpha^h(\xi)\omega) \wedge (\beta^h - \beta^h(\xi)\omega) + \omega \wedge \sum_{i,j} \frac{\partial \omega_i}{\partial x^j} x^j dx^i \quad (7.54)$$

Set:

$$\bar{\alpha}^h = \alpha^h - \alpha^h(\xi)\omega = \sum_n a_n^h dx^n$$

$$\bar{\beta}^h = \beta^h - \beta^h(\xi)\omega = \sum_n b_n^h dx^n$$

and write Equation (7.54) in local coordinates. We get:

$$\frac{\partial \omega_i}{\partial x^j} - \frac{\partial \omega_i}{\partial x^j} = \sum_{h=1}^{H-1} (a_j^h b_i^h - a_i^h b_j^h) + \omega_j \sum_n \frac{\partial \omega_i}{\partial x^n} x^n - \omega^i \sum_n \frac{\partial \omega_j}{\partial x^n} x^n$$

which can be rewritten as:

$$s_{ji} - s_{ij} = \sum_{h=1}^{H-1} (a_j^h b_i^h - a_i^h b_j^h) \tag{7.55}$$

This is condition SR$(H-1)$. The theorem is proved. □

Of course, there is no question of uniqueness. If formula (7.48) holds for $\alpha^h, \beta^h, \gamma, 1 \le h \le H-1$, it holds also for:

$$\bar{\alpha}^h = \alpha^h + \sum_{i=1}^{H-1} c_i^h \alpha^i + \sum_{i=1}^{H-1} d_i^h \beta^i + e^h \omega \tag{7.56}$$

$$\bar{\beta}^h = \beta^h + \sum_{i=1}^{H-1} u_i^h \alpha^i + \sum_{i=1}^{H-1} v_i^h \beta^i + w^h \omega \tag{7.57}$$

$$\bar{\gamma} = \gamma + t\omega + \sum_{h=1}^{H-1} e^h \beta^h - \sum_{i=1}^{H-1} w^h \alpha^h \tag{7.58}$$

provided $c_i^h = c_h^i$, $v_i^h = v_h^i$, $d_i^h = v_h^i$, $1 \le h \le H$.

This is natural moment to introduce the spaces:

$$F = \mathrm{Span}\{\alpha_h, \beta_h, \omega, \gamma \mid 1 \le h \le H-1\} = \{\sigma \mid \sigma \wedge (d\omega)^H = 0\} \tag{7.59}$$

$$E = \mathrm{Span}\{\alpha_h, \beta_h, \omega \mid 1 \le h \le H-1\} = \{\sigma \in F \mid \sigma \wedge \omega \wedge (d\omega)^H = 0\} \tag{7.60}$$

$F(x)$ has dimension $2H$ and $E(x)$ has dimension $2(H-1)$. Both are differential ideals. It follows from formulas (7.59)–(7.60) that we can choose for the $\bar{\alpha}_h$ any set of $(H-1)$ linearly independent 1-forms in E, and for γ any 1-form in F (note, however, that these choices cannot be made independently) .

7.2.6 The Concave Darboux Theorem

We finally address the problem of economic integration. The following result is due to Ekeland and Nirenberg (2002). We shall say that a smooth function V is *strongly concave* if the second derivative D^2V is a negative definite matrix; it is *increasing* if it is increasing with respect to all variables. The space E has been defined in formula (7.60), and we denote by $H \subset E$ any $(H-1)$-dimensional subspace containing ω :

$$H = \mathrm{Span}\{\alpha_1, \ldots, \alpha_{H-1}, \omega\}$$

Theorem 7.20. A necessary and sufficient condition for a smooth 1-form ω to be decomposable as $\omega = \sum \lambda_h dV^h$, $1 \le h \le H$, for some positive functions λ_h and some strongly concave functions V^h is that:

(a) condition $\mathrm{SR}(H-1)$ holds, and
(b) there is a $(H+1)$-dimensional subspace $H \subset E$ containing ω such that the bilinear form

$$(\zeta, \eta) \longmapsto \sum_{i,j} \frac{\partial \omega_i}{\partial x^j} \zeta_i \eta_j := \langle \Omega \zeta, \eta \rangle \qquad (7.61)$$

is symmetric and negative definite on $H^\perp$.

Note that this is the only result in this section which is coordinate-dependent: both the property to be characterized, namely the concavity of the V^h, and its characterization by condition (b) depend on the choice of a particular coordinate system.

The necessary part is easy. In the local coordinate system where the V^h are strongly concave, the relation $\omega = \sum \lambda_h dV^h$ yields:

$$\omega_i = \sum_{h=1}^{H} \lambda_h \frac{\partial V^h}{\partial x^i}, \quad 1 \le i \le N$$

$$\frac{\partial \omega_i}{\partial x^j} = \sum_{h=1}^{H} \frac{\partial \lambda_h}{\partial x^j} \frac{\partial V^h}{\partial x^i} + \sum_{h=1}^{H} \lambda_h \frac{\partial^2 V^h}{\partial x^i \partial x^j}, \quad 1 \le i, j \le N$$

Take $V := \mathrm{Span}\{DV^h \mid 1 \le h \le H\}$, which is indeed H-dimensional. On $V^\perp$, the bilinear form (7.61) becomes:

$$\sum_{i,j} \frac{\partial \omega_i}{\partial x^j} \zeta_i \eta_j = \sum_{h=1}^{H} \lambda_h \frac{\partial^2 V^h}{\partial x^i \partial x^j} \zeta_i \eta_j$$

and the right-hand side is indeed symmetric and negative definite.

The sufficiency part is a local result, meaning, as always, that it holds on some unspecified neighborhood of a given point. It was first proved by Chiappori and Ekeland (1999a) in the case when the ω^n are real analytic (more about this later), and then by Ekeland and Nirenberg (2002) in the case when they are only C^2. We refer to the original papers for the proof. It is also proved that, if (b) holds, the V^h can be chosen to be increasing.

In the particular case of microeconomic models, where the Walras law holds, we can express the necessary and sufficient condition in terms of the Slutsky matrix given by (7.44).

Corollary 7.4. Suppose that ω satisfies $\sum \omega_n x^n = 1$. The two following conditions are equivalent:

(a) we have $\omega = \sum \lambda_h dV^h$, $1 \leq h \leq H$, with positive λ_h and strongly concave V^h;
(b) the Slutsky matrix $S(x)$ is the sum of a symmetric, negative definite matrix and a matrix of rank $(H-1)$.

Proof. From the definition (7.44) of the Slutsky matrix, we have:

$$\frac{\partial \omega_i}{\partial x^j} = s_{ij}(x) + \omega_j(x)\gamma_i(x)$$

where $\gamma_i(x) = \sum_{n=1}^{N} (\partial \omega_i / \partial x^n) x^n$. Denote by Ω the matrix $(\partial \omega_i / \partial x^j)$, and by $\gamma \otimes \omega$ the matrix $(\omega_j \gamma_i)$; the equation can be rewritten as:

$$\Omega = S + \gamma \otimes \omega$$

If (a) holds, then, so does condition $\text{SR}(H-1)$ and we can write

$$S = Q + \sum_{h=1}^{H-1} \beta^h \otimes \alpha^h \tag{7.62}$$

with $Q(x)$ symmetric. As we noted at the end of the preceding section, we can choose the α^h to be any $(H-1)$ linearly independent covectors in the space E defined by (7.60). Consider now the subspace

$H = \text{Span}\{\alpha_1, \ldots, \alpha_{H-1}, \omega\}$ satisfying condition (b) in Theorem 7.20, and choose the corresponding α^h. Substituting the last equation into the preceding one, we get:

$$\Omega = Q + \sum_{h=1}^{H-1} \beta^h \otimes \alpha^h + \gamma \otimes \omega$$

For any $\xi \in H^\perp$, we have:

$$\langle \Omega\xi, \xi \rangle = \langle Q\xi, \xi \rangle$$

because the two additional terms on the right-hand side vanish. Since $\langle \Omega\xi, \xi \rangle$ is negative, so is $\langle Q\xi, \xi \rangle$. This shows that the restriction of Q to $H^\perp$ is negative definite. To conclude, we rewrite Equation (7.62) as follows:

$$S = \left(Q - c \sum_{h=1}^{H-1} \alpha^h \otimes \alpha^h \right) + \sum_{h=1}^{H-1} \left(\beta^h - c\alpha^h \right) \otimes \alpha^h$$

for some large constant $c > 0$. The first term is symmetric and negative definite, and the second term has rank $(H-1)$. This proves condition (b).

Conversely, suppose condition (b) holds. Then we have:

$$\Omega = Q + \sum_{h=1}^{H-1} \beta^h \otimes \alpha^h + \gamma \otimes \omega$$

where Q is symmetric and negative definite and the $\alpha^h, 1 \leq h \leq H-1$ all belong to E. Setting $H = \text{Span}\{\alpha_1, \ldots, \alpha_{H-1}, \omega\}$, it follows that the restriction of $\langle \Omega\xi, \eta \rangle$ to $H^\perp$ is symmetric and negative definite. By Theorem 7.20, this proves condition (a) □

7.3 Systems of Partial Differential Equations, and Integral Manifolds

7.3.1 Systems of PDEs

7.3.1.1 General Definitions

An *ordinary differential equation* (ODE) is a relation:

$$\frac{du}{dt}(t) = F(t, u(t)) \tag{7.63}$$

for a function u of a single variable t. A *solution* of the equation on an interval (t_1, t_2) is a differentiable function $u(t)$ such that, for every t in that interval, this relation holds. The Cauchy problem consists of specifying the value of u at a point t_0 :

$$\frac{du}{dt} = F(t, u)$$
$$u(t_0) = u_0$$

It is well-known that if the function F is continuous in the two variables (t, u), then there exists an interval (t_1, t_2) containing t_0 such that the Cauchy problem has a solution (Peano's theorem). If in addition the function F is locally uniformly Lipschitz with respect to u, that is, if there exists some $\varepsilon > 0$ and some $k > 0$ such that:

$$|F(t, u^1) - F(t, u^2)| \leq k|u^1 - u^2| \quad \text{for} \quad |t - t_0| < \varepsilon$$

then the solution to the Cauchy problem is unique (this is the Cauchy–Lipschitz theorem). These theorems extend easily to the case of systems, that is, when u (and F) take values in $\mathbb{R}^N$.

A *partial differential equation of the first order* (PDE) is a single relation:

$$F(x, u^1(x), \dots, u^H(x), Du^1(x), \dots, Du^H(x)) = 0$$

for functions $u_h, 1 \leq h \leq H$, of N variables $x = (x^1, \dots, x^N)$, so F maps $\mathbb{R}^N \times \mathbb{R}^H \times \mathbb{R}^{HN}$ into $\mathbb{R}$. A *classical solution* of the equation on an open set $\Omega \subset \mathbb{R}^N$ is a family u_h of functions which are differentiable on Ω and such that, for every $x \in \Omega$, the relation holds. There are also many types of non-classical or *weak* solutions, depending on the equation; we will not be concerned with them. If F takes values in $\mathbb{R}^M$, with $M > 1$, we have a *system* of first-order PDEs.

A partial differential equation of the pth order is a single relation:

$$F(x, u, Du, \dots, D^p u) = 0$$

between H functions $u = (u^1, \dots, u_H)$ of N variables $x = (x^1, \dots, x^N)$, and their derivatives up to and including order p. Such an equation can always be reduced to a system of first-order PDEs, by introducing auxiliary functions and equations. For instance, a second-order equation:

$$F(x, u, Du, D^2 u) = 0$$

can be rewritten as follows:

$$F(x, u, p, Dp) = 0$$
$$\frac{\partial u}{\partial x^n} - p_n = 0$$

So systems of first-order PDEs are really the most general case. Unfortunately, there is no analogue to the Peano or to the Cauchy–Lipschitz theorem. This is probably the most surprising fact about systems of first-order PDEs, and takes a while to sink in. Let us start with two examples.

7.3.1.2 First example

Consider the system of PDEs for the single function $u(x, y)$:

$$\frac{\partial u}{\partial x} = F_1(u), \quad \frac{\partial u}{\partial y} = F_2(u) \tag{7.64}$$

where F_1 and F_2 are C^1. Suppose there is a classical solution u on some open set $\Omega \subset \mathbb{R}^2$. Then $u(x, y)$ is differentiable on Ω, hence continuous. Substituting into F_1 and F_2, we find that the functions $F_1(u(x, y))$ and $F_2(u(x, y))$ are also continuous and differentiable. The equations then tell us that the partial derivatives $\partial u/\partial x$ and $\partial u/\partial y$ are themselves differentiable, and so are the functions and it is C^2 on some open set $\Omega \subset \mathbb{R}^2$. Then:

$$\frac{\partial^2 u}{\partial x \partial y} = F_1'(u)\frac{\partial u}{\partial y} = F_1'(u)F_2(u)$$
$$\frac{\partial^2 u}{\partial y \partial x} = F_2'(u)\frac{\partial u}{\partial x} = F_2'(u)F_1(u)$$

We have similar relations for $\partial^2 u/\partial x^2$ and $\partial u/\partial y^2$; the right-hand sides are all continuous functions of (x, y), so in fact u is C^2. It follows that cross-derivatives must be equal: $F_1'(u)F_2(u) = F_1(u)F_2'(u)$, and so $F_1(u)/F_2(u)$ must be a constant.

If F_1/F_2 is not a constant function, then the system (7.64) has no solution. Two remarks about that:

- System (7.64) can be written as $Du = F(u)$, with $F = (F_1, F_2)$. It is the formal analogue of the ODE (7.63): at every point we relate the value of the derivative to the value of the function. We can even formulate a Cauchy problem by specifying a point (x_0, y_0) and a value $u(x_0, y_0) = u_0$. But this time there will be no solution, unless F_1/F_2 satisfy a compatibility condition, namely that F_1/F_2 is constant.

- On the other hand, if this compatibility condition is satisfied, there will be a unique solution to the Cauchy problem, that is, a solution $u(x, y)$ of (7.64), defined in a neighborhood of (x_0, y_0), and such that $u(x_0, y_0) = u_0$.

7.3.1.3 Second example

The preceding example can be extended to more general systems. Whenever a function u appears in several first-order PDEs, then expressions for $\partial^2 u/\partial x^i \partial x^j$ and $\partial^2 u/\partial x^j \partial x^i$ can be derived, and equating them will yield compatibility conditions. Unfortunately, such compatibility conditions are not the only obstacle to the existence of classical solutions. At this point, we need to introduce a new concept.

In 1957, Hans Lewy gave the following example of two first-order PDEs for two unknown functions u^1 and u^2 of three variables (x^1, x^2, x^3):

$$\frac{\partial u^2}{\partial x^1} + \frac{\partial u^1}{\partial x^2} - 2x^1 \frac{\partial u^1}{\partial x^3} + 2x^1 \frac{\partial u^2}{\partial x^3} = f(x^3) \tag{7.65}$$

$$\frac{\partial u^2}{\partial x^2} - \frac{\partial u^1}{\partial x^1} - 2x^1 \frac{\partial u^1}{\partial x^3} - 2x^1 \frac{\partial u^2}{\partial x^3} = g(x^3) \tag{7.66}$$

Note that this is a *linear* system, albeit with non-constant coefficients: one could hardly imagine anything simpler! However, Hans Lewy showed that there are C^∞ functions f and g such that this system has no classical solution on any open subset $\Omega \subset \mathbb{R}^3$. More precisely, he showed that a necessary and sufficient condition for classical solutions to exist is that f and g are not only C^∞, but analytic. We shall give a precise definition of analyticity later on. At this point, let us only point out that, since classical solutions do exist for certain right-hand sides, the fact that they do not for other right-hand sides cannot be attributed to an incompatibility between the two left-hand sides.

7.3.1.4 The case of a single equation: the method of characteristics

Both the above examples concern systems: a single first-order PDE always has a classical solution. It can be solved by the so-called *method of characteristics*, which we explain here in the case when the equation is linear in the derivatives, but which extends to the non-linear case.

Consider the PDE:

$$\sum_{n=1}^{N} f^n(x,u)\frac{\partial u}{\partial x^n} = f^0(x,u) \tag{7.67}$$

for a single function u of N variables $x = (x^1, \ldots, x^N)$, together with the boundary condition:

$$u(0, x^2, \ldots, x^N) = g(x^2, \ldots, x^N) \tag{7.68}$$

The functions $f^n(x^1, \ldots, x^N, u)$ and $g(x^2, \ldots, x^N)$ are given and C^1. In other words, we are seeking a classical solution $u(x^1, \ldots, x^N)$ of (7.67) which takes the prescribed value g on the hyperplane $x^1 = 0$.

With Equation (7.67), we associate the system of ODEs:

$$\frac{dx^n}{dt} = f^n(x,y), \quad 1 \leq n \leq N \tag{7.69}$$

$$\frac{dy}{dt} = f^0(x,y) \tag{7.70}$$

The solutions $(x^1(t), \ldots, x^N(t), y(t))$ of this system are called the *characteristic curves* of Equation (7.67).

Lemma 7.21. If $u(x)$ is a classical solution of Equation (7.67), and if $(x(t), y(t))$ is a characteristic curve such that $y(0) = u(x(0))$, then $y(t) = u(x(t))$ for all t

---

Proof. Consider the function $\varphi(t) := y(t) - u(x(t))$. Differentiating, we find:

$$\frac{d\varphi}{dt} = f^0(x(t), y(t)) - \sum_{n=1}^{N} \frac{\partial u}{\partial x^n}(x(t))\frac{dx^n}{dt}$$

$$= f^0(x(t), y(t)) - \sum_{n=1}^{N} \frac{\partial u}{\partial x^n}(x(t)) f^n(x, y)$$

$$= f^0(x(t), \varphi(t) + u(x(t))) - \sum_{n=1}^{N} \frac{\partial u}{\partial x^n}(x(t)) f^n(x(t), \varphi(t) + u(x(t)))$$

Since $x(t)$ is known, this is a differential equation for $\varphi(t)$. We have $\varphi(0) = 0$ by assumption. Note that $\varphi(t) = 0$ is a solution, since u satisfies Equation (7.67). By the uniqueness part of the Cauchy–Lipschitz theorem, this is the only solution. □

In other words, if a classical solution $u(x)$ exists, satisfying the boundary condition, then we can compute its value $y(t)$ along any characteristic curve from its value on the hyperplane $x^1 = 0$ by solving the system (7.69) and (7.70). This suggests a procedure for solving the boundary-value problem (7.67) and (7.68), at least locally, that is, in some neighborhood of some point $\bar{x} = (0, \bar{x}_0^2, \dots, \bar{x}_0^N)$:

- for every $(x_0^2, \dots, x_0^N)$ close to $(\bar{x}_0^2, \dots, \bar{x}_0^N)$, solve the boundary-value problem:

$$\frac{dx^1}{dt} = f^1(x, y), \quad x^1(0) = 0$$
$$\frac{dx^n}{dt} = f^n(x, y), \quad x^n(0) = x_0^n, \quad 2 \le n \le N$$
$$\frac{dy}{dt} = f^0(x, y)$$

- set $u(x(t)) = y(t)$

This procedure will actually yield a classical solution in a neighborhood of $\bar{x}$, provided that the characteristic curves are not tangent to the hyperplane $x^1 = 0$, that is:

$$f^1(\bar{x}, g(\bar{x})) \neq 0 \tag{7.71}$$

We can then apply the inverse function theorem to show that the map $(t, x_0^2, \dots, x_0^N) \longmapsto (x^1, x^2, \dots, x^N)$ is locally invertible and C^1 in both directions, and prove the following:

Proposition 7.22. Suppose $\bar{x} = (0, \bar{x}_0^2, \dots, \bar{x}_0^N)$ is such that $f^1(\bar{x}, g(\bar{x})) \neq 0$. Then the boundary-value problem (7.67) and (7.68) has a classical solution in some neighborhood of $\bar{x}$.

With every $(x_0^2, \dots, x_0^N) \in \mathbb{R}^{N-1}$, we associate the Cauchy problem:

$$\frac{dx^1}{dt} = f^1(x, y), \quad x^1(0) = 0$$
$$\frac{dx^n}{dt} = f^n(x, y), \quad x^n(0) = x_0^n, \quad 1 \leq n \leq N$$
$$\frac{dy}{dt} = f^0(x, u), \quad y(0) = g(x_0^2, \dots, x_0^N)$$

Denote its solution by $(x^1(t), \dots, x^N(t), y(t))$. Substituting into (7.67), we get:

$$\sum_{n=1}^{N} \frac{dx^n}{dt} \frac{\partial u}{\partial x^n} = \frac{dy}{dt}$$

7.3.1.5 Systems: the analytic case

For systems, as we saw, the situation is much more delicate. The only general existence theorem that we know requires that the functions be, not only C^1, or even C^∞, but analytic, which is much more demanding.

Definition 7.7. A function $f: \mathbb{R}^N \longrightarrow \mathbb{R}$ is *analytic* at a point $\bar{x}$ if its Taylor expansion at $\bar{x}$ is convergent, and $f(x)$ is the sum of its Taylor series within the radius of convergence . It is analytic on an open subset Ω if it is analytic at every point $x \in \Omega$. A map $\varphi = (\varphi_1, \dots, \varphi_N)$ is analytic if every φ_n is analytic

---

In the particular case of one variable, $N = 1$, for f to be analytic at $\bar{x}$, it is required that we have:

$$f(x) = f(\bar{x}) + \sum_{n=1}^{\infty} \frac{1}{n!} \frac{d^n f}{dx^n}(\bar{x})(x - \bar{x})$$

where the right-hand side has a non-zero radius of convergence. All analytic functions are C^∞. On the other hand, there are C^∞ functions which are not analytic. For instance, the function $f(x) = \exp(-1/x^2)$ is C^∞, and it is easily seen that it vanishes with all its derivatives at the origin vanish. So the right-hand side is zero, while $f(x)$ obviously in non-zero. So $f(x)$ is not analytic.

For analytic functions, we have the very powerful (and very old) theorem which is due to Augustin Cauchy and Sofia Kowalewska. It concerns systems of H first-order PDEs for H unknown functions $(u^1, \ldots, u^H)$ of N variables $(x^1, \ldots, x^N)$ which can be put in the following form:

$$\frac{\partial u^h}{\partial x^1} = f^h(x, u, \frac{\partial u}{\partial x^2}, \ldots, \frac{\partial u}{\partial x^N}), \quad 1 \leq h \leq H \tag{7.72}$$

where x stands for $(x^1, \ldots, x^N)$, u stands for $(u^1, \ldots, u^H)$ and $\partial u/\partial x^n$ stands for $(\partial u^1/\partial x^n, \ldots, \partial u^H/\partial x^n)$.

Theorem 7.23. Consider the system (7.72), with the boundary condition:

$$u^h(0, x^2, \ldots, x^N) = b^h(x^2, \ldots, x^N) \tag{7.73}$$

Assume all the functions f^h and b^h are analytic in some neighborhood of $\bar{x} = (0, \bar{x}_0^2, \ldots, \bar{x}_0^N)$. Then, the boundary-value problem (7.72) and (7.73) has a unique analytic solution in some neighborhood of $\bar{x}$.

The proof consists of expanding the functions in Taylor series near $\bar{x}$, identifying the unknown coefficients (this is relatively easy), and then proving that the Taylor series one gets for $(u^1, \ldots, u^H)$ are convergent (this is difficult).

As an application of the Cauchy–Kowalewska theorem, we can prove that the Lewy system (7.65) and (7.66) has solution when the right-hand side (f, g) is analytic. It is enough to write it in the form (7.72)

$$\frac{\partial u^2}{\partial x^1} = f(x^3) - \frac{\partial u^1}{\partial x^2} + 2x^1 \frac{\partial u^1}{\partial x^3} - 2x^1 \frac{\partial u^2}{\partial x^3}$$

$$\frac{\partial u^1}{\partial x^1} = -g(x^3) + \frac{\partial u^2}{\partial x^2} - 2x^1 \frac{\partial u^1}{\partial x^3} - 2x^1 \frac{\partial u^2}{\partial x^3}$$

The theorem then tells us that, for any point $\bar{x} \in \mathbb{R}^3$, and any pair of analytic functions (h^1, h^2) of two variables, there is a neighborhood Ω of $\bar{x}$ and an analytic solution $(u^1, u^2)$of the Lewy system (7.65) and (7.66), such that $u^1(\bar{x}^1, x^2, x^3) = h^1(x^2, x^3)$ and $u^2(\bar{x}^1, x^2, x^3) = h^2(x^2, x^3)$.

Note that not all systems of first-order PDEs can be written in the Cauchy–Kowalewska form (7.72), that is, with the derivative with respect to the first variable singled out on the left-hand side. For a starter, there must be exactly as many equations as unknown functions. Even so, this may seem a very general result with wide applicability. Unfortunately, there are several drawbacks. First of all, it is local (but so are the results obtained by the method of characteristics). Second, and more important, the solution to the boundary-value problem (7.72) and (7.73) is highly sensitive to any changes in the equation itself or to the boundary value. For instance, if a sequence h_i^h of analytic functions converges uniformly to $h^h, 1 \leq h \leq H$ when $i \longrightarrow \infty$, together with all its derivatives, then the solution $(u_i^1, \ldots, u_i^H)$ of the problems:

$$\frac{\partial u_i^h}{\partial x^1} = f^h(x, u_i, \frac{\partial u_i}{\partial x^2}, \ldots, \frac{\partial u_i}{\partial x^N}), \quad 1 \leq h \leq H \tag{7.74}$$

$$u_i^h(0, x^2, \ldots, x^N) = b_i^h(x^2, \ldots, x^N) \tag{7.75}$$

do not converge to the solution $(u^1, \ldots, u^H)$ of (7.72) and (7.73) in general. This is what mathematicians call an *ill-posed problem*. For such problems, the solution depends from the data (the equation itself and the boundary condition) in a discontinuous manner, so there is very little hope of developing reliable numerical algorithms, and of calibrating parameters, if any.

7.3.2 Integral Manifolds

7.3.2.1 Exterior differential systems

We are now going to look at systems of PDEs from another angle: instead of looking directly for the functions which solve the system, we shall be looking for their graphs, which are submanifolds of a space with higher dimension. This is basic idea behind the notions of integral manifold and exterior differential system, which we will now explain.

Definition 7.8. An *exterior differential system (EDS) in* $\mathbb{R}^L$ is a system of equations:

$$\omega^h = 0, \quad 1 \le h \le H$$

where the ω^h are differential forms in $\mathbb{R}^L$, with possibly different degrees. If all the ω^h have degree one, the system is called *linear*. We shall say that a submanifold $\mathcal{M} \subset \mathbb{R}^N$ is an *integral manifold* of the system if the restrictions of all the ω^h on $\mathcal{M}$ vanish identically:

$$i_{\mathcal{M}}^* \omega^h = 0, \quad h = 1, \dots, H$$

Here $i_{\mathcal{M}}: \mathcal{M} \to \mathbb{R}^L$ is the injection, and $i_{\mathcal{M}}^* \omega^h$ denotes the pullback of ω^h on $\mathcal{M}$ (which in this case is just the restriction), as defined in Equation (7.19) and (7.20).

The basic example of an exterior differential system is as follows. Consider a system of J first-order PDEs in $\mathbb{R}^N$ for H unknown functions:

$$f^j(x, u^1(x), \dots, u^H(x), Du^1(x), \dots, Du^H(x)) = 0, \quad 1 \le j \le J \tag{7.76}$$

Introduce the space $\mathbb{R}^N \times \mathbb{R}^H \times \mathbb{R}^{HN}$, and in that space denote the coordinates by (x^n, v^h, p^ℓ), with $1 \le n \le N$, $1 \le h \le H$, $1 \le \ell \le H$, and $p^\ell \in \mathbb{R}^N$ for every ℓ. In that space, we consider the EDS:

$$f^j(x, v^1, \dots, v^H, p^1, \dots, p^H) = 0, \quad 1 \le j \le J \tag{7.77}$$

$$\sum_{n=1}^{N} p_n^h dx^n = dv^h, \quad 1 \le h \le H \tag{7.78}$$

Lemma 7.24. If $(u^1(x), \dots, u^H(x))$ is a classical solution of (7.76)on $\Omega \subset \mathbb{R}^N$, then the graph:

$$\mathcal{M} := \{(x, u^h(x), Du^h(x)) \mid x \in \mathbb{R}^N\}$$

is an integral manifold of the EDS (7.77), (7.78).

Proof. If we substitute:

$$v^h = u^h(x) \quad \text{and} \quad p_n^h = \frac{\partial u^h}{\partial x^n}(x)$$

in Equations (7.77) and (7.78), we get an identity, which is precisely the definition of an integral manifold □

What about the converse? We have to be a little bit careful: not every integral manifold of the EDS (7.77) and (7.78) is the graph of a solution of the PDE system (7.76). First, it must have the appropriate dimension, namely N, second, it must project non-trivially on $\mathbb{R}^N$ (more precisely, the first projection $\mathbb{R}^N \times \mathbb{R}^H \times \mathbb{R}^{HN} \to \mathbb{R}^N$ must be invertible), so that $(x^1, \ldots, x^N)$ can serve as (local) coordinates. We formalize this requirement in the following definition:

Definition 7.9. An integral manifold of the EDS:

$$\omega^h = 0, \quad 1 \leq h \leq H \tag{7.79}$$

$$dx^1 \wedge \cdots \wedge dx^N \neq 0 \tag{7.80}$$

is an integral manifold $\mathcal{M}$ of Equation (7.79) such that the restriction of $dx^1 \wedge \cdots \wedge dx^N$ on $\mathcal{M}$ does not vanish:

$$i^*_{\mathcal{M}}(dx^1 \wedge \cdots \wedge dx^N) \neq 0 \tag{7.81}$$

Denote by π_N the projection $\pi : (x^1, \ldots, x^L) \to (x^1, \ldots, x^N)$ from $\mathcal{M}$ to $\mathbb{R}^N$ and by $D\pi_N$ its derivative. Suppose condition (7.81) is satisfied near $\bar{x} = (\bar{x}^1, \ldots, \bar{x}^L)$. This means that $D\pi_N$ has full rank, namely N, so that $(x^1, \ldots, x^N)$ can be taken as a local coordinate system for $\mathcal{M}$ near $\bar{x}$. We can then prove the converse of the preceding lemma:

Lemma 7.25. Suppose $\mathcal{M}$ is an integral manifold of the EDS:

$$f^j(x, v, p) = 0, \quad 1 \leq j \leq J$$

$$\sum_{n=1}^{N} p_n^h dx^n = dv^h, \quad 1 \leq h \leq H$$

$$dx^1 \wedge \cdots \wedge dx^N \neq 0$$

near a point $(\bar{x}, \bar{v}, \bar{p}) \in \mathcal{M}$. Then there are functions $(u^1(x), \ldots, u^H(x))$ defined near a neighborhood of $\bar{x}$, such that:

$$f^j(x, u^1(x), \ldots, u^H(x), Du^1(x), \ldots, Du^H(x)) = 0, \quad 1 \leq j \leq J$$

$$u^h(\bar{x}) = \bar{v}^h, \quad Du^h(\bar{x}) = \bar{p}^h, \quad 1 \leq h \leq H$$

Proof. We have seen that $(x^1, \ldots, x^N)$ can be taken as a local coordinate system on $\mathcal{M}$ near $(\bar{x}, \bar{v}, \bar{p})$. This means that the v^h and the p^h_n functions of $(x^1, \ldots, x^N)$:

$$v^h = u^h(x^1, \ldots, x^N), \quad p^h_n = p^h_n(x^1, \ldots, x^N)$$

The relation $dv^h = \sum p^h_n dx^n$ then means that $p^h_n = \partial u^h / \partial x^n$. Hence the result. □

7.3.2.2 The simplest case

The simplest case is the one when there is a single first-order differential form:

$$\omega := \sum_{i=1}^{L} \omega_i(x) dx^i = 0 \tag{7.82}$$

The geometric interpretation of this EDS is as follows. We are given at each point $x \in \mathbb{R}^L$ a hyperplane $H(x)$ defined by:

$$H(x) := \left\{ \xi \mid < \omega(x), \xi >= \sum_{i=1}^{L} \omega_i(x) \xi^i = 0 \right\} \tag{7.83}$$

This is a *hyperplane field*, very similar to a vector field: instead of attaching a vector to every point in $\mathbb{R}^L$, we attach a hyperplane. We are used to finding integral curves of vector fields, that is, denoting the vector field by $\xi(x)$, smooth curves $x(t)$ such that $\xi(x(t))$ is tangent to $x(t)$ for every t. In a similar fashion, it is natural to ask for integral hypersurfaces of a hyperplane field, that is, denoting by the hyperplane field by $H(x)$, submanifolds $\mathcal{M}$ of dimension $(L - 1)$ such that, $H(x)$ is tangent to $\mathcal{M}$ at every point $x \in \mathcal{M}$. In other words, denoting by $T_x\mathcal{M}$ the tangent hyperplane to $\mathcal{M}$ at x, and using the definition (7.83) of $H(x)$, we want:

$$< \omega(x), \xi >= 0, \quad \forall \xi \in T_x\mathcal{M} \tag{7.84}$$

which is precisely saying that $i^*_{\mathcal{M}}\omega = 0$. So we are looking for $(N - 1)$-dimensional integral manifold of (7.82).

If such integral manifolds exist, the hyperplane field $H(x)$ will be called *integrable*. It is a remarkable fact that not all hyperplane fields are integrable, except in dimension $L = 2$, where hyperplanes are just lines, so vector fields coincide with hyperplane fields and integral hypersurfaces are just integral curves. However, in $L = 3$ already, planes are different from lines, and plane fields will not be integrable in general. In fact, as the following theorem states, the integrability condition is precisely the Frobenius condition.

Theorem 7.26. Suppose $\omega(\bar{x}) \neq 0$. The following conditions are equivalent:

(a) There is a function $V(x)$, defined in a neighborhood of $\bar{x}$, such that $Df(0) \neq 0$ and, for every h small enough, the hypersurface:

$$\mathcal{M}_h = \{x \mid V(x) = h\} \tag{7.85}$$

is an integral submanifold of the EDS (7.82).

(b) $\omega \wedge d\omega = 0$ at $\bar{x}$.

Proof. If condition (b) is satisfied, we can write $\omega = \lambda dV$ for some function V with $DV(\bar{x}) \neq 0$ since $\omega(\bar{x}) \neq 0$. If we define the hypersurface $\mathcal{M}$ by Equation (7.84), then the tangent hyperplane $T_x\mathcal{M}$ is just the orthogonal complement of the vector $DV(x)$, so that $< \omega(x), \xi >= \lambda < DV(x), \xi >= 0$ for every $\xi \in T_x\mathcal{M}$. This proves (7.84) and hence implies (a). Conversely, suppose condition (a) is satisfied. Then the vector $DV(x)$ clearly is orthogonal to $T_x\mathcal{M} = H(x)$, so that dV must be collinear to $\omega(x)$ by (7.84). It then follows from the Frobenius theorem that $\omega \wedge d\omega = 0$ on some neighborhood of $\bar{x}$ □

7.3.3 The Cartan–Kähler Theorem

7.3.3.1 Necessary conditions

We now go back to the general EDS:

$$\omega^h = 0, \quad 1 \leq h \leq H \tag{7.86}$$

Recall that the ω^h are differential forms of any order. Given a point $x \in \mathbb{R}^L$, the Cartan–Kähler theorem will give necessary and sufficient conditions for the existence of an integral manifold containing x. The proof (which we will not provide) relies heavily on the Cauchy–Kowalewska theorem, so we will have to assume that all the functions that appear are analytic.

Necessary conditions are easy to find. Assume an integral manifold $\mathcal{M} \ni x$ exists, and let N be its dimension. Then its tangent space at x, denoted by $T_x\mathcal{M}$ is N-dimensional, and the restrictions of the $\omega^h(x)$ to $T_x\mathcal{M}$ must all vanish. Any subspace $E \subset T_x\mathcal{M}$ with this property will be called an *integral element* of system (6) at x. The set of all N-dimensional integral elements at x is denoted by

$$G^N(x) = \left\{ E \left| \begin{array}{ll} E \subset T_x M, & \dim\ E = N \\ i_E^*\omega^h(x) = 0, & 1 \leq h \leq H \end{array} \right. \right\}$$

By definition, $\mathcal{M}$ is an integral manifold if $T_x\mathcal{M} \in G^N(x)$ for all $x \in \mathcal{M}$. Our first necessary condition is now clear:

Condition 7.1. $G^N(x) \neq \oslash, \quad \forall x$

In other words, if we are to find N-dimensional integral manifolds, integral elements of the appropriate dimension must exist at every point. The second condition, as we are to expect after the examples of non-existence that we gave earlier, is a compatibility condition between the original system (7.86) and its exterior derivative:

$$d\omega^h = 0, \quad 1 \leq h \leq H \tag{7.87}$$

Any integral manifold of (7.86) is also an integral manifold of (7.87), so the Equations (7.87) should also be taken into consideration when looking for integral elements. For instance, if there are N-dimensional integral elements for (7.86), but none of them is an integral element for (7.86), then integral manifolds for (7.86) cannot exist: this is tantamount to saying that the compatibility conditions with higher derivatives are not satisfied.

Therefore, we shall have to assume that any integral element for (7.86) is also an integral element for (7.87). In other words, the second equation in (7.87) must be derived from (7.86) by *algebraic* relations, not only by differentiation. Recalling Definition 7.6, we state our second necessary condition as follows:

Condition 7.2. Span$\{\omega^1, \ldots, \omega^H\}$ is closed under differentiation.

If this is satisfied, we will say that the EDS (7.86) is *closed.*

Unfortunately, conditions (7.1) and (7.2) are not sufficient. We give two counter examples to show that an additional condition is needed

7.3.3.2 A first counter example

Consider two functions f and g from $\mathbb{R}^L$ into itself, with $f(0) = g(0) \neq 0$, and $f(x) \neq g(x)$ for $x \neq 0$. Define α^i and $\beta^i, 1 \leq i \leq L-1$, by

$$\alpha^i = f^i(x)dt - dx^i, \quad \beta^i = g^i(x)dt - dx^i$$

and consider the exterior differential system in $\mathbb{R}^L$:

$$\alpha^i = 0, \beta^i = 0, \quad 1 \leq i \leq L-1$$

α^i and β^i generate a differential ideal, and there is an integral element at $0 \in \mathbb{R}^L$, namely the line carried by $(1, f(0)) = (1, g(0))$, so $G^1(0) \neq \oslash$. However, finding an integral manifold of the initial system containing 0 amounts to finding a common solution of the two Cauchy problems:

$$\frac{dx}{dt} = f(x), \quad x(0) = 0$$
$$\frac{dx}{dt} = g(x), \quad x(0) = 0$$

which does not exist in general. The problem clearly is that the equality $f(x) = g(x)$ holds at $x = 0$ only. So we need a regularity condition which will exclude such pathological situations — technically, that guarantees that the required equality hold true at *ordinary points*, a concept we now formally define.

7.3.3.3 A second counterexample

Let us work in $\mathbb{R}^2$, and let us find all functions $\phi(x, y)$ which can be written as

$$\phi(x, y) = f(x) + g(y)$$

It is well known that a necessary and sufficient condition for such a decomposition to be possible, at least for smooth ϕ, is that the cross derivative vanishes:

$$\frac{\partial^2 \phi}{\partial x \partial y} \equiv 0 \tag{7.88}$$

Consider the exterior differential system in $\mathbb{R}^4 = (x, y, f, g)$:

$$\frac{\partial \phi}{\partial x} dx + \frac{\partial \phi}{\partial y} dy = df + dg \tag{7.89}$$

$$0 = df \wedge dx \tag{7.90}$$

$$0 = dg \wedge dy \tag{7.91}$$

Any two-dimensional integral submanifold $\mathcal{M}$ of this system will be the graph of a pair of functions (f, g) which will solve the problem, provided only that it is not vertical, that is, that neither dx nor dy vanish on $\mathcal{M}$. Let us try to find such an integral submanifold. The system is obviously closed. We then look for non-vertical integral elements, at 0 say. They are defined by a set of linear equations:

$$df = A_1 dx + B_1 dy$$

$$dg = A_2 dx + B_2 dy$$

and plugging them into the system, we get

$$B_1 = 0, \quad A_2 = 0, \quad A_1 = \frac{\partial \phi}{\partial x}(0,0), \quad B_2 = \frac{\partial \phi}{\partial y}(0,0)$$

So there is a tow-dimensionl integral element at every point (x, y, f, g) in $\mathbb{R}^4$. However, there is no two-dimensional integral submanifold, unless condition (7.88) is satisfied.

7.3.4 The Cartan Condition.

If all the $\omega_h(x)$ are 1-forms, the regularity condition is clear enough: the dimension of the space spanned by the $\omega^h(x)$, $1 \leq h \leq H$, should be constant (which is obviously not the case in the counterexample above). Note that, locally, this dimension can only increase, that is, the codimension can only decrease.

If some of the ω^h have higher degree, the regularity condition is more complicated. It is expressed in the following.

Pick a point $x \in \mathbb{R}^L$; from now on, we work in the tangent space $V = T_x\mathbb{R}^L$. Let $E \subset V$ be an N-dimensional integral element at $\bar{x}$. Pick a basis $\alpha_1, \dots, \alpha_N$ of V^* such that:

$$E = \{\xi \in V \mid <\xi, \alpha_i> = 0, \quad \forall i \geq N+1\}$$

For $m \leq L$, denote by $\mathcal{I}(m,d)$ the set of all ordered subsets of $\{1, \dots, m\}$ with d elements. Denote by d_h the degree of ω^h. For every h, writing $\omega^h(x)$ in the α_i basis, we get

$$\omega^h(x) = \sum_{I \in \mathcal{I}(L,d_h)} c_I^h \, \alpha_{i_1} \wedge \cdots \wedge \alpha_{i_{d_h}}.$$

In this summation, it is understood that $I = \{i_1, \dots, i_{d_h}\}$. Since $\omega^h(x)$ vanishes on E, each monomial must contain some α_i with $i \geq N+1$. Let us single out the monomials containing one such term only. Regrouping and rewriting, we get the expression:

$$\omega^h(x) = \sum_{J \in \mathcal{I}(L,d_h-1)} \beta_J^h \wedge \alpha_{j_1} \wedge \cdots \wedge \alpha_{j_{d_h-1}} \ + \text{remainder}$$

where β_J^h is a linear combination of the α_i for $i \geq N+1$, and all the monomials in the remainder contain $\alpha_i \wedge \alpha_{i'}$ for some $i > i' \geq N+1$.

Define an increasing sequence of linear subspace $H_0^* \subset H_1^* \subset \cdots \subset H_N^* \subset V^*$ as follows:

$$\begin{aligned} H_N^* &= \text{Span}[\ \bar{\beta}_J^h \ |1 \leq h \leq H,\ J \in \mathcal{I}(N, d_h - 1)] \\ H_{N-1}^* &= \text{Span}[\ \bar{\beta}_J^h \ |1 \leq h \leq H,\ J \in \mathcal{I}(N-1, d_h - 1)] \\ H_0^* &= \text{Span}[\ \bar{\beta}_J^h \ |1 \leq h \leq H,\ J \in \mathcal{I}(0, d_h - 1)] \end{aligned}$$

The latter is just the linear subspace generated by those of the $\omega^h(x)$ which happen to be 1-forms. We define an increasing sequence of integers $0 \leq c_0(x,E) \leq \cdots \leq c_N(x,E) \leq N$ by:

$$c_i(x,E) = \dim\, H_i^*$$

We are finally able to express *Cartan's regularity condition.* Denote by $\Gamma_N(\mathbb{R}^L)$ the set of all N-dimensional subspaces of $\mathbb{R}^L$ with the standard (Grassmannian) topology: it is known to be a manifold of dimension $N(L-N)$. Denote by G^N the set of all (x,E) such that E is an N-dimensional integral element at x. Note that G^N is a subset of $\mathbb{R}^L \times \Gamma_N(\mathbb{R}^L)$

Condition 7.3. There is some neighborhood Ω of (x, E) in $\mathbb{R}^L \times \Gamma_N(\mathbb{R}^L)$ such that $G^N \cap \Omega$ is a submanifold of codimension

$$c_0(x, E) + \cdots + c_{N-1}(x, E)$$

If this condition is satisfied, we shall say that (x, E) is *ordinary* in the sense of Cartan.

In the simple case when all the ω^h are 1-forms, denote by $d(x)$ the dimension of the space spanned by the $\omega^h(x)$. Then $c_i(x, E) = d(x)$ for every i, and (x, E) is ordinary if $G^N \cap \Omega$ is a submanifold of codimension $Nd(x)$ in $\mathbb{R}^L \times \Gamma_N(\mathbb{R}^L)$. This implies that, for every x' in a neighborhood of x, the set of $E \in G^N(x')$ (integral elements at x') has codimension $Nd(x)$ in $\mathbb{R}^L \times \Gamma_N(\mathbb{R}^L)$. It can be seen directly to have codimension $Nd(x')$. So $d(x) = d(x')$ in a neighborhood of $\bar{x}$: this is exactly the regularity condition we wanted for 1-forms.

In the general case, if (x, E) is ordinary, the numbers c_i will also be locally constant:

$$c_i(x', E') = c_i(x, E) = c_i, \quad \forall (x', E') \in \Omega.$$

The (non-negative) numbers

$$\begin{aligned} s_0 &= c_0 \\ s_i &= c_i - c_{i-1}, \quad \text{for} \quad 1 \leq i < N \\ s_N &= n - N - c_{n-1} \end{aligned}$$

are called the *Cartan characters*. We shall use them later on.

7.3.4.1 The Cartan–Kähler theorem

Theorem 7.27. Consider the exterior differential system:

$$\omega^h = 0, \quad 1 \leq h \leq H$$

Assume that the ω^h have analytic coefficients and that $Span\{\omega^1, \ldots, \omega^H\}$ is closed under differentiation. Let $\bar{x}$ be a point and let $\bar{E}$ be an N-dimensional integral element at $\bar{x}$ such that $(\bar{x}, \bar{E})$ is ordinary. Then there is an N-dimensional analytic integral manifold $\mathcal{M}$, containing $\bar{x}$ and such that:

$$T_{\bar{x}}\mathcal{M} = \bar{E}$$

To conclude, let us mention the question of uniqueness. There is no uniqueness in the Cartan–Kähler theorem: there may be infinitely many analytic integral manifolds going through $\bar{x}$ and having $\bar{E}$ as a tangent space at $\bar{x}$. However, the theorem describes in a precise way (not given here) the set of all possible integral manifolds. Loosely speaking, each of them is completely determined by the (arbitrary) choice of s_m analytic functions of m variables, the s_m being the Cartan characters

To illustrate the use of this theorem, let us go back to the second counter example. There is only one integral element at every point, so that G^2 is a point in $\Gamma_2(\mathbb{R}^4)$ which has dimension $2(4-2) = 4$. So its codimension is 4.

Let us now compute the Cartan characters. There is just one 1-form in the system, namely (7.89), so $c_0 = 1$. The integral element is defined by $\alpha_3 = \alpha_4 = 0$, where $\alpha_3 = df - (\partial\phi/\partial x)(0,0)dx$ and $\alpha_4 = dg - (\partial\phi/\partial y)(0,0)dy$. Set $\alpha_1 = dx$ and $\alpha_2 = dy$ to get a basis. Substituting in the 2-forms (7.90) and (7.91), we get:

$$0 = \alpha_3 \wedge \alpha_1,$$
$$0 = \alpha_4 \wedge \alpha_2$$

so that $H_1^* = \text{Span}\{\alpha_1, \alpha_2\}$ and $c_1 = 2$. We get $c_0 + c_1 = 3 < 4$, so the Cartan condition is not met, although conditions (7.1) and (7.2) are. This is why there is no existence.

Acknowledgments

We are endebted to an anonymous referee for useful comments, and to Heriberto Tapia for a patient re-reading of a former version. Financial support from the NSF (grant SBR 0532398) is gratefully acknowledged.

References

Aloqeili, M. (2004), 'The generalized Slutsky relations'. *Journal of Mathematical Economics* **40**, 71–91.

Andreu, J. (1982), 'Rationalization of market demand on finite domains'. *Journal of Economic Theory* **28**(1), 201–204.

Attanasio, O. and V. Lechène (2009), 'Efficient responses to targeted transfers'. working paper, UCL.

Browning, M., F. Bourguignon, P. A. Chiappori, and V. Lechene (1994), 'Incomes and outcomes: A structural model of intra-household allocation'. *Journal of Political Economy* **102**, 1067–1096.

Browning, M. and P. A. Chiappori (1998), 'Efficient intra-household allocations: A general characterization and empirical tests'. *Econometrica* **66**, 1241–1278.

Browning, M., P. A. Chiappori, and A. Lewbel (2005), *Estimating Consumption Economies of Scale, Adult Equivalence Scales, and Household Bargaining Power.* Mimeo, Boston College.

Browning, M., P. A. Chiappori, and Y. Weiss, *Household Economics.* Cambridge University Press, forthcoming.

Bryant, R., S. Chern, R. Gardner, H. Goldschmidt, and P. Griffiths (1991), *Exterior Differential Systems.* MSRI Publications (18), Springer-Verlag.

Cherchye, L., B. De Rock, and F. Vermeulen (2007), 'The collective model of household consumption: A nonparametric characterization'. *Econometrica* **75**(2), 553–574.

Chiappori, P. A. (1988a), 'Nash-bargained household decisions: A comment'. *International Economic Review* **29**, 791–796.

Chiappori, P. A. (1988b), 'Rational household labor supply'. *Econometrica* **56**, 63–89.

Chiappori, P. A. (1992), 'Collective labor supply and welfare'. *Journal of Political Economy* **100**, 437–467.

Chiappori, P. A. and O. Donni (2006), *Learning From a Piece of Pie: The Empirical Content of Nash Bargaining*. Mimeo, Columbia University.

Chiappori, P. A. and I. Ekeland (1997), 'A convex darboux theorem'. *Annali della Scuola Normale Superiore di Pisa* **4.25**, 287–297.

Chiappori, P. A. and I. Ekeland (1999a), 'Aggregation and market demand : An exterior differential calculus viewpoint'. *Econometrica* **67**(6), 1435–1458.

Chiappori, P. A. and I. Ekeland (1999b), 'Disaggregation of excess demand functions in incomplete markets'. *Journal of Mathematical Economics* **31**, 111–129.

Chiappori, P. A. and I. Ekeland (1999c), 'Disaggregation of excess demand functions in incomplete markets'. *Journal of Mathematical Economics* **31**, 111–129.

Chiappori, P. A. and I. Ekeland (2000), 'Corrigendum to 'Disaggregation of excess demand functions in incomplete markets''. *Journal of Mathematical Economics* **33**, 531–532.

Chiappori, P. A. and I. Ekeland (2004), 'Individual excess demand'. *Journal of Mathematical Economics* **40**, 41–57.

Chiappori, P.-A., B. Fortin, and G. Lacroix (2002), 'Marriage market, divorce legislation and household labor supply'. *Journal of Political Economy* **110**(1), 37–72.

Chiappori, P. A. and B. Salanié (2000), 'Empirical applications of contract theory: A survey of some recent work'. invited lecture, World Congress of the Econometric Society; forthcoming in *Advances in Economics*, M. Dewatripont and L. Hansen, eds.

Debreu, G. (1974), 'Excess demand functions'. *Journal of Mathematical Economics* **1**, 15–23.

Diamond, P. and M. Yaari (1972), 'Implications of the theory of rationing for consumers under uncertainty'. *American Economic Review* **62**, 333–343.

Diewert, W. E. (1977), 'Generalized Slutsky conditions for aggregate consumer demand functions'. *Journal of Economic Theory* **15**, 353–362.

Donni, O. (2003), 'Collective household labor supply: Non-participation and income taxation'. *Journal of Public Economics* **87**, 1179–1198.

Duffie, D. (1992), 'The nature of incomplete security markets'. In: J.-J. Laffont (ed.): *Advances in economic theory (6th World Congress)*. Econometric Society Monographs, Cambridge University Press, pp. 214–262.

Duflo (2003), 'Grandmothers and granddaughters: Old age pension and intra-household allocation in South Africa'. *World Bank Economic Review* **17**(1), 1–25.

Ekeland, I. and N. Djitte (2006), 'An inverse problem in the economic theory of demand'. *Annales de l'Institut Henri Poincaré "Analyse non linéaire"* **23**, 269–281.

Ekeland, I. and L. Nirenberg (2002), 'The convex Darboux theorem'. *Methods Appl. Anal.* **9**, 329–344.

Epstein, L. G. (1981), 'Generalized duality and integrability'. *Econometrica* **49**, 655–678.

Fong, Y. and J. Zhang (2001), 'The identifiability of unobservable independent and spousal leisure'. *Journal of Political Economy* **109**(1), 191–202.

Fortin, B. and G. Lacroix (1997), 'A test of neoclassical and collective models of household labor supply'. *Economic Journal* **107**, 933–955.

Galasso, E. (1999), *Intrahousehold Allocation and Child Labor in Indonesia*. Mimeo, BC.

Geanakoplos, J. and H. Polemarchakis (1980), 'On the disaggregation of excess demand functions'. *Econometrica* pp. 315–331.

Kapan, T. (2009), 'Essays on household bargaining'. PhD Dissertation, Columbia University.

Laisney, F. (2004), 'Welfare analysis of fiscal and social security reforms in Europe: Does the representation of family decision process matter?'. *Review of Economics of the Household*, (forthcoming).

MacGill, M. and M. Quinzii (1997), *Incomplete Markets*. Vol 1, MIT Press.

Mantel, R. (1974), 'On the characterization of aggregate excess demand'. *Journal of Economic Theory* **7**, 348–353.

Mantel, R. (1976), 'Homothetic preferences and community excess demand functions'. *Journal of Economic Theory* **12**, 197–201.

Mantel, R. (1977), 'Implications of economic theory for community excess demand functions'. Cowles Foundation Discussion Paper no. 451, Yale University.

Mas Colell, A. (1977), 'The recoverability of consumer's preferences from market demand behavior'. *Econometrica* **45**(6), 1409–1430.

Rubalcava, L. and D. Thomas (2000), *Family Bargaining and Welfare*. Mimeo RAND, UCLA.

Scotchmer, S. (2002), 'Local public goods and clubs'. In: A. J. Auerbach and M. Feldstein (eds.): *Handbook of Public Economics, vol. 4*. Elsevier.

Shafer, W. and H. Sonnenschein (1982), 'Market demand and excess demand functions'. In: K. Arrow and M. Intriligator (eds.): *Handbook of Mathematical Economics*. vol 2, chapter 14, North-Holland.

Sonnenschein, H. (1973), 'Do Walras' identity and continuity characterize the class of community excess demand functions'. *Journal of Economic Theory* **6**(4), 345–354.

Thomas, D., D. Contreras, and E. Frankenberg (1997), *Child Health and the Distribution of Household Resources at Marriage*. Mimeo RAND, UCLA.

Tobin, J. (1952), 'A survey of the theory of rationing'. *Econometrica* **20**, 521–553.

Townsend, R. (1994), 'Risk and insurance in village India'. *Econometrica* **62**, 539–591.

Vermeulen, F. (2005), 'And the winner is... An empirical evaluation of two competing approaches to household labour supply'. *Empirical Economics* **30**(3), 711–734.

CPSIA information can be obtained at www.ICGtesting.com
Printed in the USA
LVOW101915301211

261846LV00001B/43/P

9 781601 982889